I0221287

Independent Filmmaking
Secrets of the Craft

Scott Shaw

Buddha Rose Publications

Independent Filmmaking:
Secrets of the Craft
Copyright © 2009 by Scott Shaw
www.scottshaw.com
ALL RIGHTS RESERVED

Rear Cover Photograph of Scott Shaw
by Hae Won Shin
Copyright © 2009—All Rights Reserved

This book contains material protected under International and Federal Copyright Laws and Treaties. Any unauthorized reprint or use of this material is prohibited. No part of this book may be reproduced or transmitted in any form or by any means, electronic or mechanical, including photocopying, recording, or by any information storage and retrieval system without express written permission from the author or publisher.

First Edition 2009
Second Edition 2026

ISBN-10: 1877792497
ISBN-13: 9781877792496

Library of Congress Control Number:
2009928378

10 9 8 7 6 5 4 3 2 1
Printed in the United States of America

Independent Filmmaking
Secrets of the Craft

Table of Contents

FADE IN:

Introduction

As a reader, I always enjoy learning the primary premise of a book in the first few lines. To this end, and to rapidly provide you with as much initial information as possible, what you will learn from this book are proven techniques that can actually get your independent film made in the most refined and expedient manner possible.

This being stated, as a person desiring to make a film, you will have undoubtedly seen that there are an untold number of books about filmmaking out there. What most of these books provide the reader with are complicated techniques that are far too intricate and costly for an entry-level independent filmmaker, with a limited budget, to ever actualize the completion of his or her film. In fact, most of these books make promises to the reader that can never be fulfilled. This book is just the opposite from that.

In this book I will provide you with the step-by-step process it takes to get your movie made, while avoiding many of the pitfalls of independent film production. This information is based upon the many experiences I have personally had in the filmmaking industry. So, the words and the experience presented in this book are as real as it gets. There will be no false promises made here.

In brief, my background is that I grew up in Hollywood, California and literally walked down _The Hollywood Boulevard of the Stars_ each day on my way to Hollywood High School. As a filmmaker I have made in excess of fifty feature films, documentaries, and music videos. And, I have no intention of stopping now. With each film I have made I have come to understand new aspects of the filmmaking process and how to make films in the most efficient manner possible. This is the knowledge and the secrets I will pass along to you in these pages.

It must be understood, however, that even though this book will detail to you proven techniques that can help you avoid many of the pitfalls in the filmmaking process—filmmaking itself is a very-very complicated process. To make a film you will be required to deal with shooting environments, scheduling, sets, equipment, and people's egos, while attempting to create your vision. Therefore, you must understand to truly realize a film, it takes a lot of focused energy. And, what I have found is that while many people desire to make a film, few have the focused energy to truly see it through to completion. Therefore, though this book will provide you with the techniques you need to get your film made, ultimately it will be you who will decide whether or not you have the wherewithal to genuinely make your filmmaking dream a reality.

Finally, in 1991 I created a new style of filmmaking that I titled, *Zen Filmmaking.* Though there are a lot of ways to describe *Zen Filmmaking;* in essence it is based upon the premise of removing as many obstacles from the filmmaking process as possible; i.e. scripts, storyboards, and even your own expectations of how a specific scene or the entire film will turn out. From this, I believe, it makes the filmmaking process as easy and as natural as possible.

This being stated, though I periodically mention *Zen Filmmaking* in the book, this text is in no way a testament to *Zen Filmmaking.* That book has already been written and published with the title, *Zen Filmmaking*. This book is about making the independent film in the best, most expedient, and pain free manner possible. Therefore, what you must do is to take what you can learn from this book, choose the formative elements you want to employ in the creation of your film, and get out there and do it.

So read this book and get out there and make your movie!

Chapter 1
Independent Filmmaking:
The Foundations

The video and later digital age dawned on us in the late twentieth century. From this, movie making has not only become much easier, but it has become much less expensive, as well. In times gone past, making a feature film was very difficult, very time consuming, and very expensive.

To give you an understanding of what it actually took to get an independent film shot just a few short years ago, let me explain the process...

First of all, you had to obtain a camera that shot 16mm film. Cameras made by Bolex, Arriflex, and Bealieu were some of the common tools of the trade for the independent filmmaker. You then had to have a tape recorder that would record your sound at the same speed as your camera. A sync-sound camera shoots at 24 fps (frames per second), so your tape recorder had to roll at that that same speed. This meant that it had to be an expensive industry deck, because the average tape recorder records at 30 fps— which would leave your dialogue out of sync with your visuals if you used a non-industry standard deck. The Nagra deck was the most commonly used reel-to-reel deck in the industry.

Then, once you had your camera and your sound recorder, you then had to buy industry standard reel-to-reel tape and the film for your camera, which is not cheap.

At the point you obtained your camera and your film, you then had to have someone on your set that actually had the understanding of how to load your camera.

It must be understood that loading film, in many of the 16mm cameras, is not easy. These cameras are not set up like a 35mm still camera, where there is a common format and they all load pretty much the same. Instead, each company that made a 16mm camera had their own unique method in which film was loaded into their cameras or their film magazines. For this reason, you had to have someone on your set that was well versed in this process, or you could not be sure if you film was actually being correctly exposed.

Once you had your film loaded and your reel-to-reel tape recorder ready to go, you then had to use a light meter to gage the lighting. You then would set your lens to the appropriate aperture in order to properly expose your film. Finally, you would then focus your lens, oftentimes using a tape measure to make sure the distance between your camera and your subject was correct. You would then put you boom operator (the man who held the microphone) in place and tell the soundman to start rolling his tape. You would call out for your camera operator to begin the camera filming. And finally, you could commence your production.

Though this was the process to get your production underway, it was hardly the end-all to getting your film ready for viewing.

The problem with film is that once you have gone through this entire process, staged and lighted your scenes, rehearsed your actors, and got your equipment up and running, you would never know what your film actually captured until you would take it in for development—which is also very expensive. Once it was developed you would then take it to the telecine machines where you could finally begin to view it. Many times, however, there would be a scratch on the film, the color would be off, the exposure would be incorrect, and you would be left with less than acceptable footage—which would then cause you to either have to reshoot the footage or pull the plug on your production due to budgetary constraints.

If you found your film footage to be acceptable, then you would need to sync it to your audio dialogue. This process entailed either transferring both your film and your audio to Beta or One Inch tape, if you planned to perform a video edit. Or, you would need to transfer your audio to mag stock and then make copies of your film footage so they could be edited upon film on a moviola.

This was only the beginning of the process, however, because once you would go through all of this you would still need to edit your project, which would either take place via an off-line video process where you would have to find someone who knew how to use the specific tape equipment you were employing or by hiring a professional film editor who could then provide you with a frame-by-frame, scene-by-scene film edit. Then, once all of this was accomplished you would still have to add sound effects and a soundtrack to your film.

Think about it… How easy it is now to make a movie when all you have to do is get a filming location, a cast, a digital video camera, a microphone, and a computer. With these few things you can pretty much do it all yourself.

But, wait a minute! Where should you shoot your film? How will you get a cast? What are you going to film? What is lighting a scene for camera? And, how can you get your actors' performances to be convincing? Well, read on and hopefully you will find the answers to those questions…

Chapter 2
Peering into the Craft

Having the desire to make a movie and actually possessing the ability to make one are two very different things. So many people are out there thinking, hoping, desiring, and talking about making a film, but few ever actually create one. And, those who begin the process, more often than not, shut down their production before their film ever gets completed. Plus, there are, of course, an untold number of armchair film critics out there who continually claim, *"I could make a better movie than that."*

But, of course, these is just the ramblings of a person who does not possess the dedication, desired focus, or ability to even begin the process of making a feature film. As such, they are not even worth discussing in this chapter.

As an educator, when I am teaching seminars or university courses on filmmaking, time-and-time again, I come across the same stories about how people run into the same obstacles, which keep them from actualizing their desire of creating a film.

What is the reason for this? The most common reason is that many would-be filmmakers:

1. *Do not learn from their own mistakes.*

2. *Do not learn from the mistakes of others.*

Therefore, in this chapter I hope to address some of the issues that are commonly encountered by independent filmmakers, to help you sincerely get out there and complete the feature film, film short, documentary, or music video that you hope to create. Because, believe me, there is no mistake that you could make that has not been made by numerous filmmakers before you!

The Digital Age

With the dawning of the digital age, filmmaking has become very affordable. Digital video cameras are relatively cheap and virtually every new computer, both MAC and PC alike, come complete with movie making software and DVD authoring capabilities. Though this has definitely added to the ease of film production, there has not been an enormous rise in the percentage of films actually being completed. Though logic would tell you this should be the case—it is not.

When I first began my path as a filmmaker, the process of filmmaking was very expensive. The 35mm, 16mm, or even Professional Super 8mm cameras were expensive. Plus, the film for them was expensive. Once you shot your film then you had to have it developed, which was also expensive. In association with this, you had to have an expensive tape recorder in order to record your sound. Then, you had to sync all of your sound to your film, either by transferring it to Beta or One Inch tape or by transferring your sound tape to 16mm mag stock and then syncing it in the final stages of postproduction. This entire process was very expensive.

The most common problem encountered, in regard to actually completing your movie, when shooting your project on film, is the fact you never know what you have until the film has been developed. Sometimes everything is fine, but other times you are left with unusable footage. This has killed many a production.

With the dawning of the digital age, much of this problem has been overcome, because you can look through the lens of your camera and, relatively, see what you are capturing. The biggest mistake people make, however, when shooting a feature film on a video camera, is that they believe the image in their viewfinder or on the camera's onboard screen is what will be seen on a T.V. or on a movie screen once the project is completed. This is not the case! These little screens are high resolution and are composed of the source image. Once you transfer that image from your camera and move it onto your computer to edit, the image is universally darker. Plus, once you output this footage to tape, DVD, or whatever other format you are planning to use for your film's dissemination, the image also becomes less refined, more pixilated, and darker.

This is the first mistake to overcome on your road to completing a feature film—learn to understand what you are truly filming and do not trust your camera's onboard viewing screen!

A simple trick to aid you in this process is to allow for a twenty percent darker image than what you are viewing on your camera's onboard screen—as this is approximately how much darker the average video image is once it is viewed on a different source than the camera's onboard screen.

Under-Lighting

Many filmmakers create dimly lighted, moody, scenes in their films to portray a specific type of atmosphere in the development of their storyline. When they light these scenes, they may use colored gels or minimal light fixtures to portray this darkness. Though the cinematographer may look at their camera's onboard screen while adjusting the lights for these scenes, what they rarely take into consideration is this twenty percent of difference between what the camera's onboard screen is projecting and what will be actually captured once the tape is transferred.

It is for this reason that I continually say, *"To be a good cinematographer you must learn to understand what the camera is viewing as opposed to what you are seeing. You must learn to separate what your human eye is seeing and what the lens is capturing."*

If you do not develop this ability, you will continually be left with less than ideal images— which is one of the primary reasons people shut down their films—because they have gone through all of the trouble to cast, stage, and shoot their movie, then when it is viewed, the photographed image is less than desirable.

It is essential that when you are lighting your scenes, no matter how dark and dramatic you want them to be, if your audience cannot see what is taking place with your actors, then all of your efforts are lost. For this reason, it is always better to open up the aperture of your camera one or two steps more than your desired end result. With this, not only have you allowed yourself the ability to compensate for the previously discussed twenty-percent but it is also very easy to bring down the light in editing programs if you feel your scene is too bright. This is not the case, however, with bringing the light up in a scene. Therefore, let the light shine in!

Speaking of Actors...

Since I mentioned actors, I guess this is a good place to talk about acting and how poor acting is one of the primary elements that kills a film—especially in the low-budget, independent market.

Why do people act badly? Because they are reciting lines that they have memorized and they do not possess the refined skills of a trained actor to actually make this process look natural. This is one of the primary reasons I created *Zen Filmmaking*—because in independent filmmaking you are commonly going to work with people who are not highly skilled actors. This being the case, though these actors may not possess the ability of a seasoned actor to spit-out memorized dialogue convincingly, they can surely say what they would naturally say, in a very convincing manner, if you tell them the subject, and then let them say what comes instinctively.

For this reason, instead of writing a script that is not only impossible to film appropriately, due to budgetary constraints, and will force your actors to memorize tons of dialogue that they cannot deliver convincingly, simply create a storyline, get your locations, go out to them, and guide your actors through their dialogue. By allowing them to be themselves, this allows them to provide your film with natural performances. And, natural is always better!

Can You Hear Me?

Bad sound is another one of the most damning elements to any film. It is one of the primary reasons that filmmakers start and then do not complete their feature. In fact, in the classes I have taught, more people have told me this is what caused them to stop production on their film than any other single element.

Just as the cinematographer must learn to capture what the lens of his camera is viewing, instead of what his eye is seeing, so too must the person who is operating the sound learn to differentiate ambient sound from what the camera is actually recording. Why? Because they are two totally different things.

First of all, what you must do is get a pair of headphones and never listen to what your actors are saying without listening to them through those headphones. In fact, it is best if you can afford a pair of external sound deadening headphones because then you will be more able to truly isolate the sound your camera is recording. If not, hold your hands over your headphones and push them closely to your ears—because if you are not isolating what is being recorded into your camera, you may emerge with a disappointing sound quality for your film.

This biggest problem you will encounter is an excess of ambient sound coming from the streets, the ocean, or the wind, depending upon where you are filming. The second biggest problem that occurs is that you will have the audio recording level turned down too low and your actor's dialogue will not be heard. So, be concise and be careful with your sound.

Finally, you must never use a camera's on-board microphone. Why? Because it will rarely isolate the dialogue of your actors. This is because of the fact that when you film actors talking, you are commonly several feet away from them—maybe more. In the space between where your onboard microphone is located and your actors are talking; there are all kinds of opportunity to pick up unwanted ambient sound. In addition, the more distance you place between your actors and the microphone, the less audible their recorded dialogue becomes. For this reason, you must get a separate microphone, plug it into your camera, with the appropriate length cable, and then get the microphone as close to your speaking actors as possible. With this, you can isolate their dialogue and remove as much ambient sound as possible.

Cinematic Style

Whereas the average filmgoer simply watches a movie, a true filmmaker studies the placement of the actors, the camera angles, the lighting, the scene staging, and the editing techniques of every movie they see. From this, they emerge with the influences to guide them to formulate their own style of cinematic creation.

The understanding gained from astutely watching every movie is what allows a filmmaker to film the scenes for their own movies in the most appropriate manner possible. Therefore, if you hope to be a filmmaker and are going to the movies to just watch a movie, you will never gain the insight of those who have walked the path of filmmaking before you.

This being stated, it is essential to realize that every filmmaking idea and cinematic techniques you have has already been done. Many people believe that with the birth of music videos, cinema was changed forever. This is not the case. Long before music videos films such as *Easy Rider, Le Mans,* and *Grand Prix,* (not to mention all of the arthouse films that were created prior to these blockbusters), laid down all of the cinematic techniques that came to define music driven cinema. So, it has all been done before. What you, as a filmmaker need to do, is study what has been done before you, learn from the mistakes, define how you can correct these mistakes, and make the cinematic image even more inviting, and then, move forward to make your own unique style of film art.

Chapter 3

Lemons to Lemonade:
What To Do
When Your Production Goes Bad

It is an inevitable fact—when you are making a film, there will be problems. Hopefully, these problems will be minor and easily overcome. Sometimes, however, these problems are much bigger and truly have the potential to derail your entire production.

The question has to be asked when these situations are encountered, _"Do I go on? Or, do I pull the plug?"_ The easy answer, oftentimes, is to pull the plug and shutdown the production. The problem with following this path is, however, then all of your money and hard work will have equaled nothing and you will not emerge with a feature film.

Problems on a film set are caused by three primary elements:

1. _Equipment_
2. _Crew_
3. _Cast_

In this chapter we will study these three variables so that you will hopefully come to better understand how to overcome any emerging problem and overcome the need for production, _"Shut down."_

Equipment

Equipment is always going to be one of the primary sources of problems on the set of any film production. As I have long said, _"In a mechanical_ *world, there are mechanical problems."* This is particularly the case with film rental equipment.

The problem with film rental equipment is that, many times, the people who rent the equipment don't care about it. From this, it gets bounced around and misused. This is common with lights, microphones, and especially cameras.

Never Loan Your Equipment

This leads us to a sidebar and the number three rule of filmmaking, *"Never loan you equipment to anyone."* Why? Because it is not their equipment and, therefore, they do not care about it, and it will often times come back to you damaged or misused.

Lights

Lights are easily tested. For this reason, it is rare that a film equipment rental company will provide you with a broken light. If you do encounter a problem with your lighting kit, this is, however, the easiest to overcome. Simply open a window or pull the shade off of a traditional light.

One of the first things you should learn about filmmaking, before you ever begin a production, is how to utilize available light and how to make the most basic of lighting fixtures work to your advantage. So, overcoming dysfunctional lighting is the easiest problem to solve.

Camera

A camera, on the other hand, is a very sensitive tool. Plus, it is very hard to test a camera for full-functionality unless it is completely put through a testing process every time it comes back to the shop from a rental. And, this is rarely the case. For this reason, many times when you rent a camera you will

24

get less than ideal results because the rental house doesn't know that there are any problems with the camera—at least until it is reported.

The problem is, if you are basing your entire production around one camera, and you find it is not working correctly; i.e. glitching, not recording, or the lens is not properly collimated if it is a film camera, it can be devastating to your production. It is even worse if you do not find this out until you are done shooting and are looking at the footage you have filmed in the past tense.

If this is the case, then, a whole day or weekend of production is gone and all of that time, energy, and money has been wasted.

Rental houses commonly offer absolutely no warrantee on their rental equipment. At most, they will offer you another day of camera usage for free. That is if they don't blame you for breaking the camera.

More importantly, what do you do if you are on the set and you have a camera problem?

In regards to the aforementioned camera rental, when Donald G. Jackson and I were filming, *The Roller Blade Seven,* a 16mm camera we had rented died early one day of the shoot. On this day, we had in excess of fifty cast members. So, we couldn't just shut down the production. The good news was Don had brought his 16mm Bolex with him. So, what we did was to shift to filming with that camera. Though not as big and professional looking as the one we had rented, it did film the footage we needed.

This is an important point to keep in mind— novice filmmakers always want to use big cameras, big microphones, big sound recording decks, as they feel it makes them look more professional. But, in today's technology, big is no longer necessary to get great results.

As demonstrated with the filming of, *The Roller Blade Seven,* it is essential to always bring a backup camera and backup microphone onto your set. Even if they are not the highest quality of equipment, at least you will have something to shoot your movie with if your primary camera or mic dies.

Mic

The microphone is one of the most essential elements of a film's production. I tell people over-and-over, *"Do not rely upon the on-board, on-camera mic if you wish to get good sound results."* Yet, time-and-time again, people don't listen. They use the on-camera mic and come away with less-than-ideal sound. In many cases, this kills their production.

I'm not going to go into a long discourse here on this subject. But, *"Don't do it!"* If you want professional quality or, at least, adequate sound, you must use an external mic. And, always use headphones to hear what your actors are saying—never listen to them without headphones, because what you hear naturally will be very different from what is captured on tape.

People

Whereas equipment is one of the primary factors that can stall a film's production—throughout my long years of experience in the independent film industry, I have found that it is much more common that people will cause a production to skid to a halt, than equipment. Now, this production halt can come in many fashions—some are unintentional, while others are much more deliberate. Let me explain a few examples…

The Crew
If the equipment is all functioning properly, then the crew is the next biggest problem on a movie set. As is the case with people not respecting other people equipment, the crew oftentimes does not care about the quality of the production. Why? Because it is not their film! Furthermore, they could care less about how much the film, or the production is costing you, because the money is not coming out of their pockets.

This is why I always suggest that you find a crew that you like and that likes you and understands what you are doing. Then, continue to work with these people. This is what I do, and I have always found it to be very beneficial.

Overall, I have been fairly lucky with my crews. But, I too have run into problems. Here are a couple of examples…

Film Reversal
Film Reversal stock is a very interesting type of film and provides a very nice finished product—particularly for a high-concept arthouse film. Loading the film in a camera's film magazine backwards and running it past the lens the wrong way, however, can provide you with less-than-ideal results.

I was helping a friend produce a film, a number of years ago, and he had brought on another friend who had shot a film for me previously, on video. The cameraman had all the credentials. He was a film school graduate and seemed to possess all the necessary skills needed to do the job. I asked him if he knew how to load and use my Arriflex 16mm camera. He claimed that he did because he had used one of them for several student projects when he was in film school. So, we went through casting, pre-production, etc. On the first day of the shoot, I brought my Arri 16mm camera, with two 400-foot magazines, and the film. The guy loaded them and we were off.

The first problem we encountered was that the cameraman left the camera's power on, between scenes, and the Arri batteries lost their charge very quickly. This sent us into a frenzy to get additional batteries and re-charge the ones we had.

The second, somewhat amusing, occurrence happened when I gave one of our actors one of my 9mm pistols to use in a scene as a prop. He was bragging to the cute girl we had cast for the female lead about how much experience he had with guns. He pulled back the slide on the pistol, as if to actually cock it, and caught the side of his finger in the chamber—which equaled tons of blood all over the place, including all over my gun. Important lesson, *"Don't let people play with props during your shoot."*

But, post all of the nonsense that went on, we completed our day of shooting. What happened next was a production killer, however. After spending all of that time, energy, and money, we took the film to *Fotokem* to be developed. When we took it to telecine, we found that the cameraman had loaded the film in the camera in the wrong direction and what we had were images that were completely color distorted.

This situation happened in the early part of the 1990s. This was prior to the digital revolution. In today's world, even if you were filming with 16mm film, like we were doing, the footage could have been shifted to Black & White and tuned-up to the degree that it would have looked just fine. But that is now and this was then…

Here is the reality about situations like this:

1. *You can let it kill your film.*

2. *You can go back up, replace the cameraman, spend a lot more money, and refilm your scenes.*

3. *You can leave the scenes as they are and add the abstract nature of the color into your film.*

…Which is what I would have done at that point in time. But, as this was my friend's directorial debut, he pulled the plug on the production. So, all the time, energy, and money equaled nothing, but the words written here upon this page.

I did, however, keep the sound tapes from my Nagra, which recorded the audio for the film, for several years hoping he would change his mind. But, when I inquired about the footage, some years later, he explained that he had thrown it away.

Never What You Expect

This leads us to the fourth rule of filmmaking, *"Things are never going to turn out the way you expected."* This is just the simple fact-of-life in filmmaking. If you do not accept this fact, and if you do not have enough money to go back, film and re-film every scene until you get it exactly the way you want it, this will bring down your production. For this reason, you have to be philosophical about the art of filmmaking and let it be art—allow the scenes of your movie to evolve and become what they are—instead of what you desire them to be.

Friends or Foes

Sometimes, in the lower budget arena of filmmaking, you will be forced to bring people onto your crew who do not possess the best credentials or filmmaking experience. This can happen for a number of reasons. The primary one is due to your budgetary constraints. The second one is based in the fact that you may want to give somebody a first-chance in the film industry and allow them the opportunity to get some actual filmmaking experience. The problem is, with few exceptions, deciding to use these less-qualified people, undoubtedly, proves to be a major mistake that will diminish the overall quality of any film they worked on.

A depictive situation recently occurred to me when I was beginning a new feature film. I hired a makeup artist I had not worked with before. He seemed to be a nice enough guy. All he wanted for his services was a *Letter of Recommendation* so he could add the film to his resume.

The problem that occurred was that all this makeup artist wanted to do was to make people look as pretty as possible. Which normally is fine. But, I had specifically told him that he would need to make one face look very bloody, as if it had been mangled in an accident. He claimed he had no problem in doing that.

It was a short shoot day; maybe four hours. By the time we were preparing to shoot the final scene, where the face needed to be made-up, the makeup artist had become very antsy. Before I even had the chance to look for it, he asked, *"Where's the blood?"* I looked and looked but could not find it. Though I knew I had brought it.

What happened was that the makeup guy did not want to do a bloody face. Therefore, he had stolen my blood and hid it in his makeup kit when I was not looking. Though I immediately realized this, in some ways I was relieved. This was because of the fact I knew he could have stolen one of my several <u>REAL</u> guns that I held in the same bag as I kept my blood. But, he did not. He just did not want to do a bloody face. Though I realized what had happened, I nicely thanked him, gave him his *Letter of Recommendation,* and let him go home—as accusations would have proven nothing. But, from his actions, one of the most essential scenes to film that day was not accomplished.

The Fact of Film Life

It is a fact-of-life, on the independent film set; you have to come to expect this type of behavior. Though you cannot ever plan for it, because you will never know where it will come from or how it will affect your production, but you must be willing to adjust your production and move forward.

This is one of the primary reasons I developed *Zen Filmmaking* and the reason I do not use scripts for my films. Because if I had to follow a script and a very-defined shooting schedule, this type of action would have destroyed my production and made me very upset. Instead, I let it go and went out and bought a new bottle of stage blood for my next day of filming.

The Budget

Many people believe that just because a film has a higher budget, problems diminish. This is not the case. In fact, in many cases, the problems amplify.

One day, Fred Olin Ray, who is a high-budget indie film Producer/Director, asked my friend Don Jackson and I to come and film some 35mm handheld footage on one of his films. Within one hour, two things occurred that could have devastated the production. The first, and least impacting, was the focus-puller for Gary Graver, who was operating the crane-cam, got his panties in a bunch and walked off the set. I offered to pull focus until a replacement would arrive. Problem solved. The second problem was much bigger, however. The camera-loader turned on the lights when he was unloading the 35mm film mags, exposing the film. He wasn't even going to tell Fred or the D.P. It was another crewmember and myself who saw the mistake and made him step up. With this, the essential scenes could be refilmed as a safety.

The Reality

This is the reality of filmmaking. You are going to have problems. No matter how much you plan, situations are going to occur that can devastate your production. Though they might not be as expensive and radical as this previously discussed situation—at any point you may feel like pulling the plug. When these situations occur, and they will occur, this is where you have to decide what you want to do—move forward, no matter what, or shut down and come out with nothing.

Believe me, as someone who has made numerous films, on virtually every project there is a moment I question, *"Is this worth it?"* But, I inevitably push on. And, this is something you will have to ultimately decide—do you want to finish your film or not?

The Cast

The cast is perhaps the most interesting element that can lead to production failure. Why? Because without a cast, you don't have a film.

The problems with cast members basically emulate from ego. This is based in the fact that virtually every actor possesses the false belief that they are going to be a star tomorrow. However, almost universally, they are not. In fact, if a person is over twenty-three years old and is not already established in the Hollywood system, it is almost impossible to, *"Make it."* At least not on the superstar level. But, you can't tell this to anybody, because they are so starry eyed and full of hopes, desires, and promises, that they will not believe you.

This is why I am completely against acting classes. (Which I will discuss further in a later chapter). The reason is, in these acting classes, the students are promised everything. That is how these acting teachers make their money—by promising people that they will make it to the stars. But, think about it. Who is teaching these classes? People who have NOT made it in Hollywood. Or, at best, people who once had a gig, no longer do, and still need to pay their rent. So, who are they to teach and promise anything?

People do not come to Hollywood to study acting. They come here to be stars. This is where the problem arises—especially for the indie filmmaker. Because these people have most likely been *an extra* on the set of a large film or television show—as this is something anyone can do and is a job very easy to obtain. But, as *an extra* they are not acting, they are just standing around. Then, when they come onto an indie set, which is generally much smaller and lower budget than that of a high-budget production, they are commonly disappointed. I cannot tell you how many times I have gone through the process of casting an actor, or more specifically actress, offering them the chance to have a leading role in a film, only to have them show up on the set and say things like, *"I didn't think it would be like this."* Or, *"I expected more."* At this stage I generally become a little indignant. Though I may not show it. If someone would say something like this to my friend, Donald G. Jackson, he would inevitably yell and scream and throw the actor off the set. But, I never thought that was the best way to handle things. From my experience, it is best to just be nice and film as many scenes with them as you can and then not expect them to come back.

Again, this is also one of the primary reasons I devised *Zen Filmmaking*—which uses no scripts. Because if the completion of your film relies upon a script, and you began to have problems with one of your actors, then you have very few options if you have to escort them off the set or if they don't come back for a second, third, or fourth day of shooting. Without a script they cannot threaten your production on any level. If they don't come back all you have to do is alter the story and finish your movie with more willing actors.

This is also the reason I suggest that if you are shooting with a person for multiple days, you always shoot a character completion scene with them on the first day. That way, if they don't come back, you will always have the means to complete their character's evolution through your film.

Most importantly, always have your actors sign a release before they ever step in front of your camera. From this, they will not have the ability to threaten you with lawsuits if they decide that they do not like your filming method or the finished movie.

People of Like Mind

When you are putting together the cast for your film it is very important that you gage the person's willingness to actually show up, be positive, and act in a film. As I have learned from experience, actors love to go to auditions, but few will show up on a set and actually act. This is due to a plethora of reasons: ego, insecurity, or the aforementioned belief that they will be, *"A Star,"* in the near future.

The problem with people who come onto a set and are negative: criticizing the production and berating the crew and other actors, is that they truly have the potential to derail your production. This is because of the fact that these people speak to the other actors, who may become engulfed in their web of negativity.

When this happens, at first, I play nice. If it continues, then I tell the person that we will not be shooting any more scenes with them on that day. I thank them and send them home. Then, I just never call them again. If they call, I explain that we had to recast their role.

The main thing is, you really need to keep your set positive. With this, many of the problems that may occur, never will, and you will be able to complete your film.

You will not always encounter negative experiences from your cast. In fact, it is normally the opposite. Many actors and actresses understand that the entire reason to be in an indie film is that it is a stepping-stone process—that by being in an indie film it will build up their resume and that it will provide them with on-set acting experience.

The best way to prevent yourself from encountering problems is to completely explain to an actor what they can expect when they come onto your set. From this, though it will not alleviate all of the potential problems with a cast member, it will shapely decrease many of them.

End Product

It is like my frequent Co-Star and Associate Producer, Kevin Thompson said to a problematic actress on the set of *Super Hero Central, "It doesn't matter what the production looks like, all that matters is the finished product."* This is very true. But, this is something that most novice actors do not understand.

In fact, to prove this point, there have been times when I have filmed an entire movie with nothing more than a handheld Sony VX2000 and a Sennheiser ME66 microphone. And, the movie turned out looking like it had a budget of a million dollars. Why? Because I used very visual locations, I knew how to shoot a movie, and my actors knew how to act for the camera.

This is an essential element to keep in mind, even if your movie is very low-budget—do not let actors and actresses, who have little experience, bring you and/or your production down. Yes, we may all want to be on multimillion dollar movie sets, but the road to that level of filmmaking is paved with well-filmed, no and low-budget films that pop.

The Worst Case

Finally, in some cases, you may have to pull the plug on your movie. This can happen for any of the above-mentioned reasons, and an untold number of others. Me, I am pretty stubborn, and I virtually never shut down a production. In the one or two times, *"Production Shut-down,"* has happened to me, what I have done is to keep all of the footage that I shot for the film, and then integrate it into another movie, once new inspiration has struck. So, *"Shut down,"* doesn't have to be a production killer. Though you may not use the footage you shot in the manner it was originally intended, you can easily rethink your project and add it to your next filmmaking experience.

Financing Your Film

It always strikes me as amusing when people contact me and ask me if I will finance their film. Their pitch is always the same, *"My movie has a great story, I have a great cast, I have had a bit part in a movie made by somebody else, so I know how to act, and therefore, I possess all of the necessary credentials and skills to go out and make a movie on my own."* I virtually never respond to these requests, because my response would not be kind. But, if I did, what I would most probably say is, *"Why should I finance your film? What's in it for me?"*

This, *"What's in it for me,"* question has to be the first thing that you have as an answer before you ever contact anyone and ask him or her for financing for a film. Why? Because this is the first question that will be asked of you and your answer must be sounder than the previously detailed logic. This is because of the fact that the answer to this question is the primary factor that is taken into consideration before a dime of film financing is ever given out.

But, we will get back to this in a moment...

The Hollywood Illusion

This leads us to the principal of the *"Hollywood Illusion."*

Budding actors and filmmakers, for whatever reason, each believe that they have something new and unique to offer. And, if they can get their name, their face, or their script, or their film out there that they will instantly be as big as Steven Spielberg, Clint Eastwood, Quentin Tarantino, or whomever.

But, they never stop to think about how many people have attempted to walk the exact same road as they want to travel. And, how many of these people have fallen flat on their face. There are multiple reasons for this. The primary one is the *"Hollywood Illusion"* itself.

There is this illusion that the successful in Hollywood are doing exactly what they want, how they want, and are keeping all of the proceeds from their actions for themselves. For anyone who has ever truly encountered Hollywood, they know, this is not the case.

Many people also believe that though it may not happen overnight, by getting their film made, the door will be opened for them, and their next film will be bigger, and the next one after that bigger still. But, let's just take a moment and think about this. How many people do you remember who were film or T.V. stars a few years ago and then faded to *never-never-land?* Or, how many people have made one film that was well received and then they have never made another one or their next film failed to make any money, so they were banished from the face of Hollywood forever?

The reality is SAG, (The Screen Actors Guild), is one of the largest unions in the world. Yet, it has the highest unemployment rate of any union on the planet. The DGA, (The Director's Guild of America), though possessing fewer members has a similar ratio. The WGA, (The Writer's Guild of America), is the same. This should let you understand that there are a lot of people out there who want to make it in Hollywood and are still out of work.

Completion

As I always say, *"Making a film is one of the most complicated and energy intensive occupations on this planet."* This is due to all kinds of reasons. First of all, and perhaps most damning, is that you have to deal with people's egos. Next, you have keep your equipment functioning, you have to get a good cast and crew, and, you have to have the money in place to make all of this happen. For these reasons and more, the majority of independent films that go into production are never completed. And, this is one of the primary reasons that people and companies are reluctant to provide financing for films—because money is given and there is no return.

Of course, you will say, *"This would never happen to my film. I will complete it!"* Well, maybe... But, the reality is, I have known a lot of new and professional filmmakers alike, who have brought projects up that have never been finished. So, your belief that your film will be completed is never enough to get you financed.

Completion Funds

From a personal perspective, I have known a number of people who have financed a film on their credit cards and then have run out of money before the footage could all be put together. Due to the fact that they have a film close to completion, they have then gone out and sought what is known in the industry as, *"Completion Funds."*

To obtain *Completion Funds* what a filmmaker does is to take the footage they have and show it to a financier. If the financier likes what he sees, he puts up the money to finish the film. But then, the filmmaker must turn the completed film over to the person who gave them the *Completion Funds,* who then sells it. The filmmaker then, commonly, becomes very upset because they never see another dime.

The Reality

Here's the reality, if you take money to make a film, or complete it, what do you think you must give the financier in return? What you must give them is the film. This is the reason they have given you money to make or complete the movie in the first place—because they want to sell your film and make money from your creative labor.

Are you going to see a dime from any of the sales they make? It is very doubtful. Why, because this is the nature of *The Hollywood Business Model*. This is how Hollywood makes money. They take the creative work of others, sell it, and keep the money.

Many people get very upset about this. But, this is the reality of the game. So, if you are going to ask someone for money, be prepared to never make a cent on your project.

You need to look at this from a philosophic perspective, if you ask and are given money to make a film. *The creative process must be your reward, not becoming a millionaire due to the sales of your film.*

The Publicity Machine

The Hollywood Publicity Machine is full of rags-to-riches stories. It always tells the tale of how this person came up with an idea, made the movie, sold it for a million dollars, and is living in the lap of luxury. One of the main things you have to realize, however, is that *The Hollywood Publicity Machine* is based upon lies, illusions, and momentary realities. And, just because it is written does not make it true. Yes, maybe a certain individual did make a film that got them noticed for a moment, but then, as previously detailed, they, more-than-likely, immediately fell back into obscurity.

What is the Answer?

The answer to the quandary about how to finance your film is simple. If you want to make a movie, the best way to do it is to finance it yourself. This way, at the end of your production, whether you complete it or not, you don't owe anybody anything. Plus, financing your own film has become much more doable in this digital age. So, there is really no reason to seek outside financing in the first place.

If you truly possess the desire and the skills to make a movie, instead of asking someone for money, you should go out there and make a film. Prove your ability. Prove that you can actually make a film, before you ask anyone for anything.

If you are still going to seek outside financing, magazines such as *Independent Film and Video Monthly* have ads in the back pages of each issue from companies that are willing to finance films. They are your best bet because this is what these companies do, finance films.

Fraudulent Finance Companies

Though I imagine the practice of fraudulent film financing has gone on since the birth of the film industry, I know it has been in practice since the rise in independent film production that took place from the 1970s forward.

What has occurred is that there have been a growing number of fraudulent filmmaking scams that have swept the globe and destroyed the hopes of many an independent filmmaker.

In essence, what occurs in fraudulent film financing is that some person or some group of individuals, sets up what appears to be a finance company designed to gain and provide financing for independent filmmakers. What happens, however, is quite the opposite.

What these companies do is to find a filmmaker who is seeking funds to make a movie. As detailed, many novice filmmakers have unrealistic expectations about the impact that their film will have. This makes them ripe for the picking for these fraudulent film-financing companies.

What these companies do is to seek out filmmakers, either through ads in industry magazines or notices placed on physical or online bulletin boards. These ads offer film financing.

Once one of these companies finds a filmmaker in need of financing, they explain that they will go about raising the capital needed for them to make their movie. How they will do this is to contact investors and offer them a percent of the film once it is completed. As most novice filmmakers believe that they have a script or a concept that will make millions, this all sounds very good.

The Small Print

What these fraudulent film financing companies generally do not tell the filmmaker is that they will keep anywhere from twenty-five to seventy-five percent of all of the money raised for their operating costs. But, in fact, they may keep much more. Why? Because they control the books. So, how can the filmmaker ever be sure about the true amount of the money collected?

Once the filmmaker is locked into a contract, what these companies then do is to contact investors from any number of sources. In many cases, what they do is known as, *"Cold Calling."* This means that they get a name, address, and telephone number of an individual by purchasing it from one of the lists made available from legally legitimate, though not necessarily morally legitimate, companies that supply the financial records of people to the highest bidder. These potential investors are then contacted and offered a percentage of the movie for a prescribed amount of money. They are, of course, promised that the film is guaranteed to be financially successful.

The reason that people are willing to invest in independent films is that everyone, across the globe, hopes to be a part of the Hollywood dream. So, even though they most likely have never heard of the filmmaker, they hope to grab a hold of the dream and be a part of Hollywood.

The contract that is given to the filmmakers is that the film financing will, *"Attempt"* to raise a specific amount of money. If they do raise the money, the sought after budget will be given to the filmmaker. If they do not, the financing company will keep all money raised and the filmmaker will be left in the position to pay back the investors even though they were given no actual funds to make the film.

A Lot of Angles

Though the previously detailed illustration is a very common practice that is employed by fraudulent film financing companies, there are many variations to this. The fact of the matter is, the minute you go to someone to raise money for your film, you place yourself in the position of financial liability. One that can truly damage your financial future.

The ultimate reality is, the toying with a filmmaker's money spans from the high to low-budget realms of the film industry. The fact is, when someone else is in charge of the bank account, you never truly know what is happening with or to the money.

This information is provided for you to raise your awareness to the types of scams that take place at the cost of the independent filmmaker. So, whenever you go and seek financing for your film, be careful! Take any contract to a valid and qualified attorney and the present all possible angles of how the contract could go back to you. From this, you will at least have a clear perspective of any deal you are entering into before you sign your John Hancock on the dotted line.

What You Owe

As previously detailed, when you take money from someone to make your film, what you owe them is either your film or the proceeds from the film. What this means is that if you owe somebody or some financial entity something, they can choose to exercise control over you and your project at any juncture.

This fact can have numerous implications, including, but not limited to, causing you to change your script, forcing you to add cast members that you had not intended on using, making you edit the film in a specific manner, or simply taking your film away from you and giving it to another Director at any stage of your production. Though this is an extreme example, I have seen this happen several times to very competent filmmakers. This is, in fact, a very common action within the world of film financing.

Ultimately, the loss to you may be your finished and final product being taken away; because what film financiers ultimately desire is not to make you a well-known filmmaker but to make money on their investment. Therefore, at the end of the day, if you take money from someone to finance your film, there is the very real possibility that you will lose control over it either during production or during distribution.

I have seen so many filmmakers become very upset by these facts. But, the fact of the matter is, they chose to overlook the obvious when they were reaching out their hand and asking for money.

For this reason, I cannot emphasize enough, if you seek outside capital for you film:

1. *Know with whom you are doing business.*

2. *Make sure that the language is very specific in all aspects of production control and film and title ownership once the project is complete.*

3. *Define any repercussions between you and your financier if your film does not find its way to completion.*

Finally, it is best to finance an independent film from your own wallet whenever it is possible. With this, no matter what the ultimate outcome, you have no one to make any excuses to and only yourself to blame and/or congratulate.

Chapter 5

Actors Are Very Average

Casting an actor for your film is one of the most important elements to the success of your project. In fact, it may be <u>THE</u> most important element because it is an actor who will portray the message you are attempting to convey to your audience.

People come here to Hollywood, California from across the globe chasing the dream of becoming a movie star. Certainly, there are actors everywhere, but Hollywood is the home of the movie industry. As such, this is also the focal point of where people direct their hopes on achieving acting success.

As someone who grew up in Hollywood, I believe I have a unique perspective of the film and television industry. Throughout my life I have been surrounded by those who have made-it in the industry, and those who wish that they could have.

Very early on in my life I came to realize that what may be defined as talent has very little to do with whether or not a person will make-it in the industry. Industry success is based more upon luck and being in the right place at the right time, as opposed to being in the wrong place at the wrong time; i.e. making bad career choices. But, more than anything else, industry success is based upon karma or destiny. This being said, everybody comes here to Hollywood believing that they will be the one that will, *"Make-it!"*

Casting

From a filmmaking perspective, it is you, the filmmaker, who must put out a casting notice, go through all of the headshots that you will receive, decide which ones to call in, and then finally decide upon which talent to cast for your film. And, I use the term, *"Talent,"* very loosely.

The Headshot

The problems with casting a film are numerous. At the root of many, if not most, of these problems is the actor. This problem begins with a headshot.

As someone who has cast numerous films and has looked at literally millions of headshots, I can tell you, *"What you see is not what you get."*

One of the most common things that people do is to send you a headshot that makes them look beautiful. This is based on several factors. It may be that the photo was taken ten years ago. Or, it may be that the photograph is highly retouched.

I believe that the primary reason this problem arises is that people, meaning actors and actresses, actually believe that they look better than they truly do. When they see a great photograph of themselves they think, *"Wow, that is how good I really look. If a photographer can make me look this good, then certainly a Director can."* But, anyone who has made a film knows, this is not the case. A film and/or particularly a video camera are very unforgiving. Though lighting can be adjusted and diffusion filters used, doing all of this takes a lot of time and energy, which equals a lot of money. And, a lot of money is something that most independent filmmakers do not have.

This *Beautiful Headshot Scenario* is particularly the case with actresses. I cannot tell you how many times I have called an actress into an audition and could not even confirm, with one hundred percent certainty, that the person sitting in front of me was the individual in the photograph. I commonly say to them, *"Wow, I would really like to meet the girl in this picture."* But, for the most part, they are so vain that they do not even get the joke. In some cases, in my earlier days, I have torn up their headshot right in front of them. But, I have learned to become more kind as the years have progressed.

The point being, never trust a photograph.

Training

The second problem you may encounter, while casting a movie, is the training an actor has undergone.

Here in Hollywood, and the surrounding area, there are literally thousands of acting coaches. People come from all across the globe to study with these people in hopes of landing a role in a film. The problem is, who are these acting coaches? With very few exceptions they are people who have come to Hollywood and have attempted to, *"Make it."* When they did not, they somehow landed a gig as an acting instructor.

Ask yourself, how many famous actors are professional acting coaches? And, the few one-time successful actors who have become acting coaches are those who fell away from favor in Hollywood and could no longer get roles. As such, they are left without any other skill than to train other people in how to act, in order to pay their rent.

The main point to understand is that acting is not about learning to act. Acting is not about studying. Acting is about being natural. This is particularly the case with acting for the camera. So, for all of these people who pay all of this money to be judged in a class by other *wanna-be* actors, they are only lying to themselves if they think acting training is any more than a way to fill someone else's pockets with cash and waste a lot of time.

The Acting Class
This being stated, I cannot tell you how many times a person's acting coach or their ongoing acting training has gotten in their way of their actually being in a film. There have been times when I have cast an actor or actress for a film and later they tell me that they cannot show up on the day of the shoot because they cannot miss their acting class. Yes, it is hard to believe. But, this has happened to not only myself but to numerous other filmmakers I know, as well.

You ask, *"Why?"* Because their acting coaches are very vehement about them never missing a class or postponing a *scene-study* they are set to present with their acting partner.

But, more than this, most acting coaches are jealous of anyone who has actually been offered a role. From this, they talk their student out of accepting it. They do this by convincing them that they have the potential to be a, *"Big Star."* Therefore, why should they appear in an indie film?

Of course, those people who have listened to their instructor and passed on the roles offered to them in indie films have never gone on to anything except pay their acting coach more money. But, these are just a couple of examples of how acting training negatively affects an actor's potential and how it may affect the outcome of your film.

Never Acted Before
Here in Hollywood and in other cities, as well, there is the major problem of people auditioning for a part in an indie film who have never acted in front

of the camera before, but they have been *an extra* on a major motion picture or television set. On these sets, they see the massive number of crewmembers doing things, the name-actors being led in from their trailers to the set. Plus, the food is great and the atmosphere is electric with high-budget film energy. They think this is how all movie sets are supposed to be. But, to the independent filmmaker, we know this is not the case.

This being said, it is very important to weed out those, *A-Picture Dreamers* from the ones who actually want to act.

It is essential to understand that it is not a bad thing to bring a person onto your set who has never acted before. In fact, from personal experiences, I have gotten some great performances from people who can just be themselves in front of the camera but never had any intention of becoming a professional actor. On the other hand, there are those who are locked into the ideology that all movie sets are major productions—where the actors will be pampered and catered to.

The reason that you do not want to cast someone like this is that they will be disappointed once they arrive on your set. This disappointment will be obvious, and it may spread to your other cast members. And, negativity spreads on a movie set very quickly. Therefore, you really need to watch out for this type of person and keep them off of your set.

The simplest remedy for this is to find out an actor's expectation if you are thinking about casting them. Ask them, *"What sets have you been on?"* If they tell you about a student film they were in or an indie project, then you have no worries. They will be fine on your set.

The Extra

On the other hand, here in Hollywood, it is very common that a person will have been *an extra* in a film and or on T.V. and they will list these roles on their resume. But, being *an extra* is not being an actor. Therefore, if their resume is made up of several of these productions—for example they list that they have several high-budget productions listed and they are not in SAG, then you know you may have a problem.

Now, this is not to say that a person who has been on a large set will not be willing to work on an indie film. But, this is a warning that you must talk to them about their expectations to alleviate any on-set misconceptions that may bring your production to a halt.

Payment

The next area that has to be addressed when casting an actor is their desire for payment. The truth of the matter is, many actors expect to be paid for their performances. But, the reality is, in most cases, especially regarding an independent film production; the novice actor does not deserve to be paid—at least not in cash.

One of the main problems, especially here in Hollywood, returns to the source point of a person who has been *an extra*. As *an extra* they were paid minimum wage, or less, for their time. Though they were most probably never seen on screen in the finished product, none-the-less, they were paid for being on a set. From this, they have developed the mindset that they deserve to be paid for any performance.

Many times, I have heard the same logic and the same statement made by *wanna-be* actors, *"You will make money from this film, why shouldn't I?"* But, as I have told so many of them, it is a much bigger issue than that. First of all, I am the one who is putting this project together and paying for it. Plus, there is no guarantee that this film will make any money at all. Moreover, I explain to them that there are other ways to be paid, than only by being paid in cash. For example, by actually being allowed to act in a film they have the opportunity to be seen and possibly utilized by other filmmakers. Plus, they will be provided with the opportunity to learn about camera placement, hitting their marks, and refining their acting skills in front of a camera.

Oftentimes, these statements do not alter the mindset of those actors who possess the belief that they deserve to be paid for their performances. When this occurs, then I explain that their name means nothing to the project. And, no one will be buying this film simply to see them in it. Of course, then the belief that they will be, *"A Star,"* any day now is again voiced. *But, you are not one now…*

The fact of the matter is, I realized many years ago that it is never a good idea to pay a novice actor to be in a film. As most undiscovered actors have very little income, they come to depend upon any money that they may earn in the realms of film. If you pay them once, then they will constantly be contacting you and asking you for more work.

In reality, I have been very lucky in the many films I have created in hiring talented actors and supplying them with a copy of the film, once it was completed, as payment. The reason I detail the previously explained, less than ideal circumstances, is that it is undoubtedly a situation that each of us, as filmmakers, will come up against. I have and you probably will to.

For this reason, whenever I cast an independent film, I am very specific in the casting notice that there is no pay involved with participation in the film. The only payment is copy and credit. Of course, there are always those who show up at the audition asking, *"How much does it pay?"* But those people, I cast to the wayside.

Very Average

Probably, the most damning of all elements to any film's production is an actor's ego. As discussed, everybody comes to Hollywood assured that they will be the next, *"Big Star."* They all believe that they have the looks, the talent, and the drive to become successful.

This world has become celebrity obsessed. Everywhere, the life of the famous is broadcast, written, and spoken about. Due to this fact, actors believe that they have the potential to come to Hollywood and become just as big as the biggest name. *"If they can do it, so can I."* I have heard that statement so many times from so many *wanna-be* actors and actresses that I cannot even count the number.

But, none of them ever do make-it. Why? Because they are very-average. They are just like everyone else who comes to Hollywood. They look the same, have the same hairstyle, wear the same trendy clothing, study from the same acting teachers, and go to the same headshot photographers. But, they all go home, back to wherever they came from, never having done anything in Hollywood but, at most, to being *an extra* and showing up to auditions with headshots that don't look like themselves, spouting the promise, *"I'm a great actor."*

The ones I have known that have made-it in Hollywood, to whatever degree, are the ones that have had their own style and their own identity. They created their own niche for themselves by being who they are and not defining themselves by who they studied with or circulating beautiful headshots that they look nothing like.

Casting the Actor

We, as filmmakers, are always dependant upon the actor. We are also dominated by what is available. Meaning, we can only create our cast from the available options we are presented with. So, what is the answer?

1. Don't trust the headshots.
   Tear 'em up if the actor or actress comes to you and looks nothing like their photo.

2. Forget about where they studied.
   'The Studied' bring far too many preconceived notions and other nonsense to your set.

3. Cast people you like.
   Cast people you wouldn't mind hanging out with.

4. Never become friends.
   Don't become overly friendly with your cast, at least not while you are filming. Why? Because then the relationship becomes convoluted and

*your cast may expect more than you
are willing to give.*

5. Always tell actors what to expect.
    *Tell them where you will be filming,
    how large your crew is, what kind of
    equipment you are using, and how
    many actors they will interact with.
    With this, you prepare them for what
    is to come and they will not surprise
    you with an attitude of
    discontentment.*

Chapter 6
The Name Actor

In times gone past in independent filmmaking it was a common practice to hire one of two, depending on how much money you had, *"Name Actors"* to put in a film. And, though this practice has fallen by the wayside for the most part, it is still in practice to a certain degree.

What is a, *Name Actor?* A *Name Actor* is someone who maybe once starred in a television series, perhaps was in a number of A-films, or was a former sports star turned actor. The reason these people were employed was the fact that for you to sell your indie film, buyers wanted to be able to sell copies based upon known names in the cast. It was believed that people would only rent movies or that cable networks would only play films with a recognizable name in the cast.

The way this process would work is that the filmmaker would track down one of these individuals, pay their rate, and film them, commonly for only one day. Then their name would be placed first in the screen credits, and the poster or video box would have their name large and above the title. Oftentimes, however, these actors would be in no more than a few scenes.

The Reality

The reality of hiring *Name Actors* is, what you are hiring, for the most part, are has-been actors whose time had come and gone. As they have no other developed skills, other than acting, they are delegated to working in low or no budget films that they could care less about. What they do bring to the table is a set of acting skills that novice actors do not possess. Therefore, what you are receiving for your money is an acting performance that is commonly much better than all of the other actors in the film.

There is actually a list of these actors that circulates in Hollywood filmmaking circles. This list details the names of the actors that if you put them in a film will quite possibly assure you of adding to your sales numbers. As these names frequently change and I do not wish to insult any specific actor, I will not list their names. But, they are pretty easy to figure out just by looking at an actor's credits on the internet movie database. If they have a very long list of films they have appeared in each year—they are probably one of, *"The Listed."*

Throughout my years in the film industry, I have worked with a number of these so-called *Name Actors*. In each case I have found them to be nothing but friendly and professional. In fact, when I was first getting my feet wet in the industry, as an actor, I was allowed to work opposite an actor that I had followed throughout my youth. So, there are unseen benefits to hiring these people as part of your cast. But, using a *Name Actor* can have just the opposite effect, which I will discuss in a few moments.

Contact and Cost

In times gone past, to contact a *Name Actor* you would have to go to the *Academy Players Directory,* look up the actor you desire to hire, and contact them through their Agent or Manager. As we are now in the age of the internet, virtually every working actor has his or her own website or myspace page. From this you can alleviate the middleman and contact them directly and offer them a part in your film.

The cost for hiring these *Name Actors* runs anywhere from $300.00 to $10,000.00 per day—with the average cost between $3,000.00 and $6,000.00. Each of these actors has their own set price and they are rarely, if ever, negotiable. So, just a hint; if you are thinking about hiring one of them; don't go at them thinking that you can tell them that you are making the greatest independent film ever made and they should give you a discount because they just do not care, as they have no doubt heard that same pitch a hundred times before. They are simply doing a job that equals a prescribed payment.

The Relationship

The other thing to keep in mind is that these people do not want to be your friend. They are just getting paid to show up and do their job. So, do not hire a fallen actor or actress just because you loved them in your adolescence and you hope to become best buds.

A couple of years ago a friend of mine was looking for a *Name Actress* to put in his film. I suggested an *Academy Award Nominee* I knew. He loved the idea. So, I called her up and set up the deal for him. After his day of shooting, he continued to call her and tried to speak with her on the level of friendship. Finally, she called me and told me to tell him to quit calling her—the job was done!

So, just keep that in mind if you plan on hiring a *Name Actor*. They are not taking the job because they believe in your script or want to be your friend. They are only taking the job to equal a paycheck, as they probably have more than enough friends. So, don't confuse their mindset.

SAG

If an individual is an established actor, then they will be a member of SAG, *The Screen Actor's Guild*. When you hire a member of SAG you must shoot your film under a union contract. There is no way around it.

Though SAG will not come after you, the filmmaker, for hiring a union actor and not having the appropriate papers in place; they will go after the actor and force them to pay any monies they earned on a non-union production to the union, as well as leveling a fine against them. If these amounts are not paid, then the actor will be suspended from SAG and will not be able to work on future union projects. So, virtually no union actor will ever work in a nonunion film.

So, if you are going to go after a *Name Actor* you will need to find out if they are an active member of SAG. If they are, and you still want to use them, then you will need to become what is known as *SAG Signatory*. What this entails is initially filling the appropriate paperwork with SAG.

In recent years, with the expansion of the independent film industry SAG has expanded its contract base, making it easier and less expensive for indie productions to file for *Sag Signatory* status. This being stated, the main thing to know is that to get your film approved by SAG, you will need to have production insurance, which can be very expensive.

As SAG is a union, they want all of their members to remain safe on any set. So, the production insurance is an absolute requirement.

Do not believe that if you are in another state, other than California, that a union actor can get away with acting in a nonunion film. The SAG policy of only working union, spans the entire globe. So, do not believe that a union actor will accept a gig by telling them, *"You will be filming in Arizona, so there is no need to worry about the union."*

The final requirement of the SAG contract states that you open your books to the union. If your film actually does sell and begins to make money, it is the requirement that you pay the actors residuals. So, be prepared to do this, because if your film does make money and you do not pay the actors their residuals, SAG will legally come after you and they are a big union with deep pockets.

Financial Core

There is one exception to the rule regarding the union actor. That exception is *Financial Core Status.*

There is a little known *caveat'* in the SAG rules that states a union actor can become what is known as, *"Financial Core."* What this means is that they relinquish their full membership in the union and are allowed to work on both union and nonunion projects. The problem with this level of membership is, however, once a union actor becomes *Financial Core* they can never change this status if their career takes an upswing and become a fully unionized member again. It is for this reason that most SAG members are not *Financial Core.*

This being stated, many of the *Name Actors* who work predominately in the nonunion field have become *Financial Core.* So, this is something to inquire about when seeking out a *Name Actor* to be in your film. If they are, in fact, *Financial Core,* then you can hire them, pay them their rate, and not worry about insurance or other formalities that SAG requires.

The Reality of Name Talent

As detailed, in times gone past, it was a virtual requirement that an indie film have at least one name player in the cast. With the plethora of indie films that began to be created with the dawning of the digital age, this requirement has fallen away. The reason for this is that many of the *Name Actors* have been in so many films that they have played-out their uniqueness and their bankability. In fact, when a filmmaker uses some for these *Name Actors* their project is actually frowned upon by many of the buyers.

Today, the reality of the indie film market has changed so that *Name Actors* are no longer necessary to cause a film to sell and be embraced by the masses. In fact, it has been proven over the past two decades that the majority of the independent films have truly altered and shaped the evolving indie market so that they have had no name players in the cast. For this reason, it is ultimately up to you, if you wish to use a Name Actor in your film. You will need to decide if they are worth the money and are worth the possibility of enhanced sales potential or, in fact, the opposite—lessened sales.

For me, the sole reason I use someone who may be considered a *Name Actor* is because I have been in this industry a long time; they have become a friend, and I enjoy working with them. I never use them due to admiration or the possibility of enhanced sales. So, if you choose to use a *Name Actor,* acutely define your reasoning, make sure that it is in your budget to do so, and then give it a try—maybe they will be in your film…

Chapter 7
The Casting Couch

I am frequently asked what is the best way to cast a feature film. Though there is no hard and fast rule for this, what I can tell you is that the traditional methods of casting do not guarantee success—especially for a film made with a limited budget and geared towards the independent film market.

Casting

From a traditional perspective, what takes place when you cast a film is that you put out a casting notice for the film. In this notice, you provide the title of the film, a description of the film's storyline, and a description of the various characters you are seeking. These notices traditionally include the role, the character, the character's attributes, and the type of person that would fit said role. For example:

Role: Stephanie
Type: Co-Star
Sex: Female
Age Range: 18 – 30
Race: Caucasian
Hair Color: Blonde
Special Skills: Martial arts or dance abilities required.
Character Description: This character is a vibrant athletic and attractive female who possesses the ability to rapidly shift her mood from compassionate to sad, onto intensely angry.

Here in Hollywood, this character description would be placed in an online or hardcopy ad via the various casting services. From this, you will literally get hundreds, if not thousands, of submissions per role. Oftentimes, actors and the agents of actors will submit people that are in no way near what was detailed in the character description. This is because of the fact that it is believed that you may be seeking another, unspecified type of actor or actress. Therefore, it is believed by submitting a different character type than you have asked for, you may actually end up calling them in and possibly cast them in your film. Though this tends to be a big waste of time on the Casting Director, it is a very common occurrence. In any case, upon receiving the submissions, you and/or your Casting Director sort through them, pick out the best candidates, call them, and set up an audition.

The Audition

Traditionally, at an audition, the actor shows up at your office and reads what are called, *"Sides."* *Sides* are a scene from the upcoming movie.

The actor reads the role with either the Casting Director or a pre-production associate. Commonly what the person who is reading the *sides* with the actor does is to perform the role very flat. This is done in order to test if the actor has the ability to actually act-out the role if there is no other actor in the scene—for example if they are performing the role in a one-shot.

Once the actor has given their initial performance, the Casting Director either tells them, *"Thank you,"* and they leave or they are guided to perform the scene with a slightly different emotional emphasis.

Once the audition is completed, the *best-of-the-best* are chosen and are then brought back for what is known as a, *"Call Back."* Here, they are usually given a different scene to perform and again the best candidates are weeded out. Finally, and ultimately, this process leaves you with the best choice for the role.

One of the funny things that happens, here in Hollywood, is that many times actors are called in to audition for roles in a big film or television series. The actor becomes very excited that this may be their, *"Big Break."* The reality is, however, the role they are auditioning for has already been given to an A-List star and there is no true reason for them actually going to the audition.

Why this occurs, I don't really know. Perhaps it is to appease the unions or to make actors believe that their agent is actually doing something for them. In any case, the role will never be theirs.

This, of course, is not the case for the independent film. Independent filmmakers always want to cast the most talented and most appropriate person for the role.

Special Skills

One of the amusing things that I have seen time-and-time again when an actor submits for a role requiring a special skill such as skateboarding, roller-skating, or the martial arts, is that that the skill is listed on their resume, and they come into the audition full of promises of how well they can perform the skill. But, trust me, test them at this skill before you ever bring them onto your set or you may be very disappointed.

When I was making, *Samurai Ballet,* I needed a cast of skateboarders for a scene. This one very attractive girl came to the audition swearing up and down that she was a master skateboarder. When asked if she had brought her skateboard, she told me that she had forgotten it. But, she was nice and she was pretty, so I told her to show up the day of the shoot—which she did, without a skateboard, of course. Luckily, I had an extra one in my trunk. I gave it to her. When we were ready to shoot the scene in downtown L.A. all of the rest of the skateboard crew took off on their cue, but she fell flat on her face. After a few attempts and a lot of wasted Super 8 film, I decided to just tell her, *"Thanks, but forget it."*

Why did she do this? I don't know? But, this is a tendency in Hollywood. I guess people think that if they can show up, even though they don't have the required skills needed, that they will be given a role in the film. But, what they don't think about is how this can adversely affect the production and the cost of a production.

A perhaps more amusing situation happened to me when I was filming, *Samurai Vampire Bikers from Hell.* There were obviously a lot of martial arts in that film. So, in virtually all of the casting notices, I listed martial arts as a required skill.

This one actor came in stating he was a black belt in taekwondo. Back then, being much more trusting of the word of an actor, I cast him in a role as he had a very good look and seemed like a nice guy.

For his first scene in the film, my character, Alexander Hell, and his character were to go toe-to-toe. The scene starts off with us facing off. He kicks at my character, which dodges the kick and delivers a spinning heel kick to his face. We choreographed the scene and the camera was ready to roll.

Now, for you non-martial artists, it must be explained that a black belt would know how to easily get out of the way of an oncoming kick simply by leaning back out of its path. This is especially the case with a circular kick such as the spinning heel kick.

In any case, cameras rolled and, *"Action."* Bam, I kicked the guy right in the jaw. He didn't lean back.

I halted the scene, as I wanted to make sure he was okay. He was. He explained away the mishap and told me that it wouldn't happen again.

"Action." Bam, I kicked him in the face again. Now, this went on for five takes. I am sure he must have had a very sore jaw.

Though I felt for the guy, this is the problem with actors who lie about their special skills. And, this is a warning, to you, the filmmaker—be careful believing what an actor tells you and always test them before ever believing a word they say.

Does Traditional-Casting Work?

Previously detailed in this chapter are the methods of traditional casting. Though this process of traditional casting is pretty much what is *embedded-in-stone* in the industry, for the independent market it really leaves a lot of variables that are not encountered by the A-Film system for which it was designed.

First of all, for the high-budget, union, A-Films, every actor in Hollywood and, for that matter across the globe, is clambering to get a role. Once they have made an inroad into one of these features, not only are they well paid for their time but also instantly have bragging rights. As previously discussed, however, this is not the case with the independent film.

For the most part an actor works on an independent film either for free or for a very limited wage. Their expected payment is a role in a film, that will be finished, so that they can footage on themselves to add to the *Demo Reel;* which is one of the universal Hollywood standards whereby an actor is judged.

The problem arises in the fact that many if not most independent feature films are never completed. Therefore, an actor is never sure when or if they will ever even get to see the finished product and receive the sought after footage to add to their *Demo Reel.*

This is a good place for me to discuss this issue…

The Reality of the Independent Film

As I continually tell novice actors and actresses, *"Ninety-nine percent of the casting notices out there are bullshit. They are placed by people looking for girlfriends or boyfriends or people who hope to get laid. They are placed by people who desire to make a movie but don't have the understanding, the wherewithal, or the money to actually complete the project. Or, they are taken-out by dreamers who wish to make a film, talk about it forever, but never truly get it off the ground."* In all of these cases what happens is that an actor goes to an audition, rehearses with the cast and the Director, maybe even acts on a set for a few days, but at the end of the process, the film is never finished, and they come away with nothing but the experience.

I do not even know the number of people I have personally known who have attempted to bring up a film, gone through all of the pre-production

68

nonsense and then have it fall apart before it ever even gets close to completion. In many of these cases, I could see it coming and tried to warn them and give them advice. But, the ego is a strong force here in Hollywood and everybody believes they are making one of the greatest independent films to ever go up. So, anything I said went to deaf years. Some of these people I would bump into years later and I would ask them if they ever made their film. The answer was always, *"No."*

Now, this is the reality that actors and actresses have to deal with. Particularly actresses—especially if they are young and attractive.

What I always tell a person to do before they commit to any project is to check the filmmaker out. Have they done any other film project?

I certainly understand that everyone has to begin somewhere, and for every filmmaker there is a first film. But, credibility comes from what you have done before, not by what you are speculating that you will someday accomplish.

For this reason, I always suggest that novice actors and actresses seek out only student films when they are attempting to refine their craft and learn the ropes about acting for film. The reason for this is that a student film must be completed if the student wants to get a grade for the class. With this as the motivating factor, they are almost universally completed—where it is just the opposite with independent films.

Actor's Reality

As discussed in the chapter on actors—many actors that are new to the game falsely believe that they are destined to be a star. So, this brings us to the other side of the issue of casting the independent feature film and how casting the wrong individual can spell the loss of money and ultimately the demise of your production.

As detailed, it is not solely the ego of the actor that causes them to bring problems to your set but also everyone around them; i.e. their agent, their acting coach, their scene study partners, and their so-called friends telling them why they should not be in an independent film. From this, comes a lot of flaky behavior on the part of actors and actresses.

Honestly, I feel I have been very lucky, and I have met and cast some very talented people for the films I have created. This being said, I too have had some less-than-ideal experiences in film casting. One of the most exaggerated examples happened when Donald G. Jackson and I were about to begin shooting the original version of the movie, *Lingerie Kickboxer.*

I had come up with and developed the story of, *Lingerie Kickboxer.* This movie was to be based on a female secret agent who hid her identity as a professional kickboxer.

While we were in pre-production for the film, Don and I came up with a realization of how to get a lot of publicity for the movie. We planned to shoot the entire movie on 35mm film in only twenty-four hours. Basically, we planned to do this to prove that an entire 35mm action-adventure movie could actually be filmed in this short amount of time.

With this as our basis, we cast the movie, got our equipment in order, scheduled our crew, and had it set up that *Entertainment Tonight, Access Hollywood, the L.A. Times,* and other news sources would meet our team at various shooting locations around Los Angeles during the day of filming. It was an elaborate plan, but we felt that we were all set to go.

Our cast and crew were scheduled to meet us at our North Hollywood offices at 5:30 AM on Saturday morning, the day of the shoot. But, at 4:30 AM I received a telephone call from the actress who was scheduled to play the lead role. She told me that she could not make the shoot due to the fact that her boyfriend was having a family reunion in Fresno, California and she had to attend. Though I obviously asked her to reconsider, she had made her decision and was not going to change her mind. As we had no backup actress to put into the lead role, we had to pull the plug on the production.

This illustrates how so many people have a chance to make it in Hollywood and throw it away. This also illustrates how an actor or an actress can truly mess up the career of a filmmaker. I mean we, Don and myself, were the ones who had scheduled all the press meetings, had found and set up all of the locations, and had all of the secondary actors and actresses scheduled and ready to go. But, this all went by the wayside from the decision of this one actress.

What ultimately causes people to make this style of decision we, the filmmakers, may never know. For some actors, I suppose it is the fear of success. But, whatever the reason, this is how a production can be ruined.

As a filmmaker, the lesson I learned from this is that you can never rely on one individual, one lead actor or actress, when you are making a film. For example, if we had a second choice for the role, and had she been scheduled to be on the set, as well, perhaps in a co-starring role, then shut down of this production would have been avoided.

The sad realty of this is that a similar situation had happened to me a few years previous to this when I was making the film, *Atomic Samurai,* which ultimately was released as, *Samurai Johnny Frankenstein.* So, I should have already learned my lesson.

On the day we were shooting all of the office scenes for my character, Sam Rockmore, in an office building on Hollywood Boulevard, the actress I had scheduled to play my secretary called me up—she had been arrested and was not going to be getting out of jail in time for the shoot. Hey, at least she called me...

The problem was, this actress had a very distinctive look—very Marilyn Monroe. Due to this fact, replacing her was not going to be easy. The guy who was helping me produce the film decided to go out to Hollywood Boulevard. He was assured that he could find another actress walking down the street. He came back an hour later, empty-handed.

But then, I looked around at the actresses who were already on set, and there she was, the perfect replacement. All we did was to run down to *The Walk of Fame,* buy her a new outfit, and she became the perfect replacement. Though she had a completely different look than my jailed lead actress, which is why I didn't think of her immediately, she pulled off the role perfectly.

So, my advice for when a single role is highly definitive of your production is that you should always have a backup actor or actress ready to step-up to the plate if your lead takes a powder. You don't even have to tell them that this is the case, as this may then elevate their hopes. But, by having them on set keeps you prepared. Then, if your lead doesn't show up, for whatever reason, just tell the other actor that they have just been promoted. From this simple action, your production will always be protected.

Attitude

Some production debacles are not so intense as the previously described cases. Once an actor or particularity an actress is on the set, you may find that their attitude quickly changes. This happened to me when I was filming, *Hollywood P.D. Undercover.* I had tried to stay away from the hands-on casting of this film. I had left that to Richard Magram, who helped me put the film together.

I had met Rich who had been kicking around the industry for a number of years and was ready to get his hands into production. So, I told him the characters I was looking for. He put out a casting notice. I went through the headshots with him, and I let him make the calls.

Hollywood P.D. Undercover is one of the films I made in two days. Which I will discuss the process of later in this book.

In any case, we were shooting some of the scenes at Rich's house in the Hollywood Hills. I was downstairs preparing for the scene when I was told that there were rumblings from one of the actresses upstairs.

The scene was to be where an undercover police office walks in and discovers a brothel of prostitutes that were brought into L.A. from Shanghai. So, there were several Asian women waiting to shoot their scene in a picturesque bedroom.

Apparently, one actress didn't like the level of our production. So reluctantly, I went upstairs to see what the problem was. *"What is this, a porno?"* she exclaims.

Now, it is at this point when you, the filmmaker, can make a choice. One, you can throw this type of actor off of your set—which is what all of my instincts told me to do. Or two, you can be nice and explain the film and the filmmaking situation to her—which is what I actually did.

After I explained to her that the film was designed to have a documentary feel to it, which is why our cameraman was going handheld and there was minimal lighting, the actress immediately calmed down. In fact, she really tried to outdo all of the other actresses in the scene. So, sometimes explanation is all that it will take to calm down an unruly cast member.

The other Producers on the set, knowing me, and my temperament during a shoot, were very surprised at my calm reaction. But, for whatever reason, it is the choice I made, and it worked out for the overall presentation of the film.

Male Verses Female

There is one fact that I have learned through my years of filmmaking, *"It is easier to find a talented male actor as opposed to finding a talented female actress."*

I suppose there are numerous psychological reasons for this. Girls tend to be more vain. Every guy they meet tells them that they are beautiful. And, once in the industry, they are promised stardom. Whatever the ultimate logic for this case scenario is, you will find, as a filmmaker, that it is much easier to find a male actor who really knows his chops rather than a female actress. Plus, male actors bring far less ego and problems to a set.

Why am I telling you this? It is just to prepare you for the ultimate reality of casting. This is just the way the business works... So hopefully, this understanding will help you steer clear of potential problems.

Casting

After all of this discourse you may be asking, *"If the traditional method of casting do not work, with the reading of sides, etc., then what is the best way to cast a film?"*

There is no absolute hard and fast rule for this. So, if you want to bring in actors and *read-em,* (meaning given them *sides* and allow them to perform a scene), that is up to you. But, what I do is really simple, *"I trust my feelings."*

What this means is that I could care less where a person has studied or if they can perform a scene from a written page. What I want is a person who can be themselves on screen. I want a person who can be natural and convincing in their role.

It is for this reason that I never attempt to make a person anything other than what they are. I do not try to cast a girl who is naturally a good-girl in the role of a slut or a sensitive guy in the role of a hard, tough guy. Because by doing this, you are asking people to actually be able to act. And, what I have found, at least at the independent level of filmmaking, is that finding someone who can actually act not only takes a lot of time but, more importantly, the way a person performs at an audition is far different from the way they act once they arrive on the set. But, if all a person has to be is themselves, then this takes no skill to provide a believable performance in an acting role.

It is for this reason, if I want to cast a junky; I hire someone who has or used to have a drug problem. If I want to cast a gangbanger, I hire someone who used to be in a gang or at least grew up in an area where gangs were prevalent. If I want to cast a musician, I get someone who can actually play an instrument. And, so on... But, more than these obvious examples, I cast people who fit the ideal of the character whom they are to play. With little room for interpretation, performances become much more believable.

It is as simple as that. If you want to get believable performances in an independent film from your novice actors, hire a person who only has to be him or herself.

Chapter 8

Screenplays:
The End of the Story

Let's face facts. The stories have all been told. But, you can never convince a Screenwriter of this fact because they believe that the script they have written has captured some new and unique storyline that has never been explored. But, they are lying to themselves.

Think about it. How many films do you see each year? Now, multiply that number by ten thousand, or more, and that is how many films that are being made each-and-every year in the various countries across the globe. Plus, this is not to mention the thousands of films that have previously been produced that you had no idea were in existence.

So, no matter how unique you believe your screenplay to be. It is not. Just because you haven't seen it produced or written about before, does not mean that is the case.

This being said, throughout the history of filmmaking, filmmakers have used scripts as the basis of their production. And, I doubt this will change anytime soon.

But, for you, the independent filmmaker, you need to truly analyze the place of a screenplay in your film and how it will aid or hinder your production.

Screenplay in Hand

Before I get into the main subject of this chapter, I think a funny story may be in order...

A year or so ago, a clean 35mm print of this 1960s European horror film had surfaced and it was to be screened at a theatre on Beverly Boulevard in L.A., complete with an appearance by the original female star of the film who looked amazingly good for the years. Also scheduled was Quentin Tarantino who owned the print, had brought the actress to the States, and was to give the opening invocation. At the screening I could not even count the number of people who had arrived with a large envelope holding a copy of their *"Great"* script that they wanted to pass on to Tarantino, tucked precisely under their arm.

The funny thing, QT didn't show up. Instead, director Joe Dante took the stage. But, as he does not hold the cult standing of Tarantino no one gave him their script and most left the screening very disappointed that Tarantino had not arrived...

Understanding The Screenplay

What is a screenplay? A screenplay is a series of words that details characters that makeup a story, that tells the tale of a person, place, or thing.

How do you make a screenplay come to life? You buy or rent filmmaking equipment, hire actors, have them memorize the dialogue presented on the pages of the screenplay, film them acting out their roles, edit their performances, and output your product. Though this all sounds very logical, let's think about it...

How many independent film productions have you seen where the acting was just terrible? What is the primary cause of this? The primary cause of this is that the actors were forced to memorize dialogue and then vocalize those lines in a manner that they would never use in their actual life. In other word, they are busy being something that they are not—saying things that they would not say.

Now, there are some highly professional actors out there who can pretty much get completely into <u>ANY</u> character and speak the most obscure dialogue in the most believable manner possible. Though these actors are out there—think about it, how many times have you been watching a professional actor on television or the movie screen and their performance were completely non-believable? And, this is a professional actor! So, what can you expect from the performances of your novice actors?

Due to the limited budgets of the independent film industry, it is oftentimes very hard to find an actor willing to work on an indie film that has the developed chops to make all of their dialogue completely believable. What then is the answer? I will talk about that in a moment...

The Indie Screenplay

For a novelist, the story that they write is complete and whole onto itself. Why? Because it is told within the pages of a book. So, nothing more is needed but the imagination of the reader. A screenplay, on the other, is not whole and/or complete within itself. It is written so that talented actors in exotic and visually stimulating locations will perform it.

The problem is, particularly for the independent filmmaker, putting together enough financing to make an elaborate screenplay a reality is very difficult, if not impossible. So, before you even begin to base your indie film upon a screenplay, you need to take that fact into consideration.

What you need to realize is that though the story may play beautifully on the page, bringing it to a place of reality, where it can be filmed, is at the least very difficult. Whereas, a high-budget Hollywood production has the financial backing to make even the most elaborate screenplay a reality, the independent filmmaker does not possess this luxury. Therefore, as an independent filmmaker, the first thing you must do is to make your screenplay-based film, doable.

The high-budget Hollywood Producer seeks out and reads numerous screenplays every year. Once they find one that they like, they put the finances together to bring it into production—no matter how much that amount may be. Though this is the way it is done with high-budget films, this is not the best way to lay the foundation for an independent feature film.

First of all, instead of finding a screenplay you like and then going about finding the locations, renting them, casting the actors to fill all of the individual roles, wardrobing the actors, buying the props detailed in the story, and so forth—in independent filmmaking, it is far more advantageous to follow a completely different path. That path is to create a screenplay based around where you live, where you have to shoot, the actors and actresses you know, and the props you already possess. So, instead of basing your screenplay upon an elaborate idea, first-and-foremost, think about what you have, who you know, where you are geographically located, and then develop a story that fits into those parameters.

This does not mean that you need to think small, but what it does mean is that you need to think about creating your screenplay in relation to the locations, actors, and storyline that can be presented to an audience in a believable manner. If a movie is not believable, then no one will watch it. And, people watching your movie is what gets your name, as a filmmaker, out there and this will increase your sales—which ultimately will equal dollars in your pocket.

Success

There have been some very successful films that have been made on a very limited budget and have become very successful. Perhaps the most noteworthy of these, in recent years, is *The Blair Witch Project*. The original version of this film was shot on High-8 video in locations around where the filmmakers lived. What made this film so believable was that the cast and the locations truly embraced the feeling and the intensity that the filmmakers hoped to create. From this, though it was created with a limited budget, the film was widely embraced.

I imagine this film was made up of a lot of improvised dialogue and I will speak about that in a moment, but what the filmmakers did isolate, and capture was a truly unique experience. And, this is what you, as a filmmaker, want to use as a guide. You want to create a film that presents a unique experience to the audience. In many cases, your guidebook for doing this is your screenplay.

Screenwriter Verses Director

It is important that if you are the Screenwriter of the film that you do not try to alter the Director's vision. We have all heard stories where the Screenwriter sees what a Director is doing to his or her story and throws all kinds of fits. But, there is a simple solution to this. If you do not want your story or screenplay to be altered in any manner, than put the finances together, learn about lighting, camerawork, and audio, and go out and make your own film. If, on the other hand, your only desire is to be a part of a larger project then you can offer a screenplay you have written up for adoption by another filmmaker. If you do, however, you have to let it go, because undoubtedly there will be changes made to it by the Producer and Director.

Dialogue

Many novice Directors either write a screenplay or like one that has been written by a friend. They put the financing together to bring it up and then they begin to guide their actors down the path of saying every word, exactly as it has been written upon the page. The fact is, this causes problems.

No matter how good your sets and your staging looks; if an actor's performance is not believable it will kill your film. What is the primary reason for an actor's performance being non-believable? They are spitting out dialogue in a manner that is not natural to them.

Why does this happen? The primary reason is that they are being told that they must say everything that is written in the script.

I can tell you from personal experience that high-end film Directors do not expect the actors to say exactly what is on the page in the manner that it is detailed in the script. They allow an actor to add their own words and their own interpretation to the screenplay. In fact, what I have done when I have performed other people's written words is that I have taken my scenes and actually crossed out unnecessary words and written the dialogue to fit my style of delivery.

On television sitcom sets, this process is a little bit different. Due to the fact that they shoot multiple cameras, and their movement is based upon specific words in the dialogue, the actors must not only hit their mark, but also speak the words that are in the script. It is for this reason that on a sitcom the actors rehearse Monday through Thursday and then shoot the project on Friday in front of a live audience. But, an indie film is not a sitcom.

I have watched so many Directors take their actors through hours-and-hours of rehearsals in order to get them to spit out the dialogue exactly as it is written on the page. I have also seen these same Directors freak out when the cameras finally role and their actor's performance fall apart because they are not used to actually acting on a set, with people around, in front of a camera.

My philosophy about this is simple; let the actors say whatever they want. Now, you don't have to take this to the extreme like I do with *Zen Filmmaking,* by basing your entire production on the naturalness of having no script at all. In fact, most filmmakers can't or don't want to do this. But, what you need to do, if you hope to get natural performances, is to allow an actor to be him or herself. With this, you receive a very watchable and natural performance.

How Does it Work?

You may ask how does this work? How can I base my production upon a script and still allow my actors to say what they want?

The fact of the matter is, by directing your actors in this style makes your job much easier.

What you do is to take your script, however developed it is, give it to your cast and let them get the feel for the characters they are portraying. Then, instead of putting them through long grueling rehearsals, maybe you do one *Table Read* or maybe not. Or, maybe you simply have them show up on the set. At this point you stage your scene. You put the actors in their places and you just let them BE the character. If they say the dialogue in a natural manner as it has been written, great. If they make up most of the dialogue but stay in character, also great.

With this style of directing not only does your job become much more easy, but the performances become much more natural. From this, your film becomes much more watchable.

By directing your film in this manner, the only time you will need to correct or redirect an actor is if they are exhibiting a slightly incorrect emotion or if they have gone off on an improvisational tangent that doesn't truly fit the story. By allowing your actors to truly be a creative part of the film, empowers them. From this, you are not considered a hard taskmaster. Instead, the actors walk away from the film believing that they have truly contributed to the overall presentation of the film. With this, everybody emerges with pride about their participation in the film.

Improv

Early in my career, I too wrote screenplays to base my films upon. I quickly found out, however, that they were more of a hindrance than a positive tool in the filmmaking process. Therefore, I ceased to base my films upon a screenplay.

From a personal perspective what I do when I am creating a film is to come up with a story, put my cast together, and then write up a shot list of scenes that I believe will help to tell the story.

When I am on the set, I then, (and not before), tell the actors what the scene is about, turn on the camera, and let them have at it. From this, the performances emerge as natural and impromptu as possible. So, many times I am just amazed at what the actors have come up with to detail the back-story and the development of their characters while telling the story.

Admittedly, this style of filmmaking is not for everyone. Most filmmakers need structure. But, this being said, by creating a film in this fashion, not only do you free yourself from the hours, days, weeks, and months of creating a screenplay, but you are never disappointed in an actor's performance because you never force them into a box and expect them to say the dialogue the way it was written in your mind.

My ultimate advice for the indie filmmaker, and particularly the Director is to free yourself and make your job as pain free as possible. To achieve this, you must remove as many obstacles as possible from the filmmaking process. And certainly, we can all agree, that the constraints a script places on a production, especially when defining what is expected from the actors performing the script, is one of the easiest hindrances to overcome.

Believe me, the freer you make your production, the easier it will be to make the indie film and your cast and crew will all come away loving you and have had a positive experience.

Chapter 9
Cinematic Style

Just as the Screenwriter sets the stage for the story and the Director guides the overall artistic vision of a film, it is the individual in charge of the cinematography who must decide upon a visual style for a film.

In high-budget films, the Cinematographer or Director of Photography is commonly hired due to their extensive experience with the craft of cinematography. Due to their standing, they often have the final word upon how a film will be shot. In the independent filmmaking market, however, the Director of Photography does not hold such a dominant role. In fact, on an indie film set the cinematographer may be solely an individual under the guidance of the Director.

Director and Cinematographer

On the indie film, it is quite common that the Director guides the Cinematographer in the type of camerawork that it is actually taking place. In fact, in many cases, on low-budget productions, the same person who has written the film, is paying for the film, is directing the film, and is also the Cinematographer. Though this individual is performing many tasks, it does not necessarily diminish the overall outcome of a film. If this person is a competent cameraman, then the film has the potential of coming out with excellent cinematic quality.

Whatever the case as to who is actually guiding the camerawork on a feature film, to make that film jump out at the audience it must possess a unique cinematic style. For this reason, it is essential that you decide what, *"Look,"* you want your film to possess and go forth, from the first frame forward, onto obtaining and presenting that *Look* to your audience

There are many ways to add to the *Cinematic Look* of your film. In this chapter I will detail some of them.

Camera Technique

The first and undoubtedly the most important element of your film's cinematography is the camera technique. The right camera placement and the right movement can add a lot of production value to your film.

Most films, are shot by setting up a tripod, staging the actors appropriately in front of the camera, locking off the shot, getting focus, and then initially filming a *Wide Shot*. Once that is accomplished, the expected *One Shots* are filmed for the individual actors, and that is that. Now, if all you want to convey to your audience is a story expressed by traditional cinematography, then you will have easily accomplished your end goals. If, on the other hand, you want to be a bit more creative with the *Look* of your film, then this is where *Art* comes into play.

Art

It is essential for you, the filmmaker, to understand that the minute you include the ideology of, *"Art,"* in your film, there will be a certain group of individuals who immediately will not like your film and dismiss any merits it may possess. Why? Because *Art* is defined differently by every person. What one person likes, another person will hate.

But, if you desire to push the envelope of filmmaking, this is where *Art* comes into play. And, the filmmakers who have chosen to embrace *Art* in their cinematic presentations are the ones who have caused the craft of filmmaking to continually evolve.

Adding *Art* to you film can take on many forms. Certain dialogue, the style and actions of the actors, the costuming, and the locations are all essential elements that have the potential of enhancing the *Art* of any film. But, it will be the camera that must capture that *Art* if you hope to make it viewable to the audience. For this reason, *Film Art* is based upon cinematography.

Lighting

Lighting is one of the, if not the most, essential elements to adding a unique definition to your film. Though the process of lighting can be as natural or as elaborate as your budget and/or your personal vision dominates, lighting is what sets the stage for what style of *Film Art* you wish to illustrate to your audience.

When I am teaching classes on filmmaking I demonstrate to the class how quickly lighting can radically change the feeling of a scene. What I do is lock my camera off with a *One Shot* on a student. Of course, the student's image is then projected to the class via a television screen. Then, I have another student turn off one row of the overhead classroom lights. Instantly, the student's face goes from being overly exposed to possessing a unique and artistic shadowing.

Lighting a character for any interior scene you are shooting is literally that easy. You simply control and limit the light that is hitting their face and your scene instantly becomes artistically driven.

Controlling the Light

In high-budget films it is common that the lighting placed on the various characters is very flat and very expansive. The cinematographer and lighting techniques combine their resources and do this so that the actor is completely revealed to the audience. With this style of blanket lighting the physical atmosphere is also fully revealed.

Though high-budget film productions utilize an expansive crew and an untold number of lights to obtain any desired end-results, this really is not necessary. All you have to do is to turn on the general room lights and you will have the same effect.

If you want to isolate your characters and give them a more pronounced uniqueness in your interior scenes, however, this is when the, *"Less is more,"* understanding comes into play.

The most basic technique to provide your actor with a dramatic look is to place them in a darkened room and turn on one light—placed at the desired distance from them to one side. The light you use can be a professional light or it can be a typical household light. The distance you place it from the actor will depend solely upon how much of your character's features you want to reveal to your audience.

Many people, new to the film game, mistakenly feel that lighting a scene is very difficult. It is not. As just demonstrated, all you need is a household lamp and you can provide a scene with a very artistic feel.

Gels

One of the primary things I like to do when lighting the interior scenes in my films is to add colored gels to the lights. A colored gel is a piece of thin plastic made up of a very specific color; be it blue, red, purple, green, or whatever... Color gels come in various color intensities, and they can be purchased at virtually any photo shop and certainly online. Gels are relatively cheap and they can provide you with a very unique look to your film.

What I commonly do is to take one of my lights and place a specific colored gel over it. Then, I light up the wall behind my actors in that color. I then take another light and depending on how exposed I want my actors to be in a specific scene, I light them with a different colored gel. Though their skin tone obviously comes through, (unless I use a very dark gel), this provides the scene with a very distinctive look.

Of course, this lighting practice can be designed with many variables. You can place multiple colors on the rear wall. Or, light one wall with one color, another with a different color, and so on.

You can also use techniques such as having a specifically colored gel placed central to your scene. At a distance your actor is bathed in natural color. Then, when they walk closer into the shot, the gel takes over their lighting, and their skin tone changes to that color. This is an ideal technique when you want your actors to express a completely different mood than was projected in other scenes.

If you want the facial features of your actors to stand out, you can use a gel to light the background, while using a clear light on their face. The main thing to understand is that lighting is your choice. You can get very creative with it just by practicing with various colored gels. You can do the most elaborate color schemes, or you can just turn on a lamp. Ultimately, you have to decide what *Look* you want your film to have, pick up a few lights online or at your local photo store, and go out and play with them until you master the style of lighting you wish to use in your film.

Lighting Packages

As previously discussed, many filmmakers want to use only the biggest and most professional looking equipment. This too is the case with lighting packages.

Lighting kits for film can literally go up into the thousands of dollars per lamp. And, some indie filmmakers buy these very high-end kits to light their project.

Now, there is nothing wrong with these high-end lighting kits. But, they are not required to make your indie film look good. If you are going to use controlled lighting, all you need is a little practiced technique and the most basic of lighting fixtures.

The most basic and cheapest lighting fixtures are called, *"Photofloods."* A *Photoflood* is a lighting fixture that provides you with a socket and a light hood that mounts onto a light stand, and projects a continuous source of light. You can change and alter the amount of light a *Photoflood* projects by using a bulb with a higher or lower wattage, depending on your lighting needs. You can also add what are known as, *"Barn Doors,"* to a *Photoflood. Barn Doors,* like a door, open and close, thereby controlling the amount of light that is dispersed from your lamp onto your scene or your actors.

Photofloods and *Barn Doors* are both relatively cheap. Yet, they can provide you with great results by using them. In fact, you can purchase low-end *Photofloods* from most hardware stores for approximately $5.00.

With a *Photoflood,* you can attach gels to them with wooden clothespins, or you can use them as stand-alone lights. In either case, what you desire is for your film to present a unique look while being well lighted. *Photofloods* can answer this desire at a fraction of the cost of the high-end studio lights.

Outdoor Lighting

Controlling outdoor lighting is obviously much different than designing indoor lighting, especially for the independent filmmaker with limited resources.

An interesting example of this occurred when I was new to the film industry and working predominately as an actor. I had been cast in an episode of a television series that was to be shot at the beach. I was to walk hand-in-hand with this actress. The Cinematographer decided that there was too much sun on our faces. So, he had his crew extend an overhead sunshade, for over a thousand yards, along the beach so that the sunlight would be diffused as we walked.

Obviously, the independent filmmaker is not going to possess the resources necessary to control outdoor lighting to that degree. What the indie filmmaker has to do is to learn how to work with the available lighting elements of the outdoors and make them work to his or her advantage.

Items such as a *Bounce Card,* which is a pop-open reflector, can be purchased from photo stores. *Bounce Cards* are a great way of isolating and redirecting light onto the faces of your actors when additional light is needed.

But, more than just using external objects to control your external light, you can get great results by learning how to control the aperture on your camera's lens.

The aperture is what controls the amount of light that is allowed through your lens. By bringing this down, light is lessened. By opening it up, more light is allowed to enter. Simply by controlling the amount of light that you allow to enter your lens, you can obtain great and unique results.

As each camera is different, you will need to consult your owner's manual to see how to change your aperture from an auto-status. By learning how to do this you will be able to take control over every outdoor, (and indoor), shot. No matter how bright or how dim you find the natural light to be.

Advanced Camera Techniques

Once you have come to define the cinematic style you want to present in your feature film, you may want to think about adding movement to your scenes. To do this you will want to move the camera in the steadiest manner possible.

Virtually all of the modern cameras have what is called a steady shot. What this does is to remove that bouncing or jerking effect when the camera is moving.

If you look at old lower-budget films from the 1970s and before, you can see how jerky and shaky the camera was when the cameraman attempted to do a *"Traveling Shot."* Soon after this point in history the *Steadicam* was invented, which provided a cameraman with a harness that caused the camera to move with a much more balanced flow. From that point forward, moving or *Traveling Shots* became much more natural, and they no longer drew attention to the fact that the camera was being moved.

Today, you can get various accessories that provide the modern camera with the ability to move like a *Steadicam*. They are all relatively cheap, in and around the $300.00 range. In fact, there are several sites on the internet where they teach you how to make your own *Steadicam* using easily obtainable parts.

For the most part, however, the steady shot on your camera is all that you will need to film scenes, as you are moving. As long as you take the time to move consistently and naturally while walking, your camera alone can provide you with a great addition to the ordinary locked off shot.

The Moving Shot

Aside from walking, there are several methods that can add to the *Look* of your *Traveling Shot*. Using a very competent roller-skater is one of the best methods. What you do is to hand your camera off to a cameraman who is a very competent skater and let him film your scenes while traveling to, from, and around your actors. This is a technique I used in some of my early films, and it left the audience wondering how were able to ever capture that shot.

If you have a person who can skate very well, this is a great technique that will truly add a unique scope to your film. This is particularly the case if you are filming in an expansive environment. In this style of location, you have your skater begin filming and then skate up to your actors from a far distance and then either travel with them as they exchange dialogue or skate around them to provide a sense of constant movement.

A second method to obtaining this result is using a very competent skateboarder. There is a difference, however, when using a skateboarder compared to a roller-skater. This is based in the way a roller-skater propels himself compared to that of a skateboarder. The roller-skater moves in a very fluid and natural pattern, propelling himself with a side-to-side movement. The skateboarder, on the other hand, needs to kick off the ground from one side, every few seconds. So, if you are going to use a skateboarder, due to the fact that there are a lot more of them, than competent roller-skaters, you will need to have them train in obtaining the most natural and non-jerking forward propelling movements possible. The other alternative to this is to have them film in small segments—using only the footage where they have no need to push themselves forward and are instead, only coasting.

If you have access to a wheelchair, this is another method to obtain a very fluid moving shot. What you do is to have your cameraman sit down, get focus, and then when he is ready to begin filming your actors, you have someone push him along. With a wheelchair you can get great *Traveling Shots* of moving towards your actors and once you have arrived, stopping and allowing dialogue to take place.

Of course, there is always the *Car-Shot* to obtain a grand scene of movement in your film. This can be obtained from any number of methods. But, it works best if you have someone with a pickup truck because then your cameraman has an easier time of not being interrupted or hindered from getting his shot, compared to say if you are using a passage car for your *Camera Car,* (the car with the cameraman in it).

There are few methods that add great scope to your film if you choose to film one or more of your actors as they drive. The basic shot is to have your

Camera Car pull up next to the car where your action is taking place and then driving along side of it as your cameraman films it. You can do the same thing by having your *Camera Car* in front of the primary vehicle, while your actor drives forward.

Though your production may not have the ability to record dialogue while filming these shots, what you can do is use them as an establishing shot. Ideally, you will shoot the car traveling in a unique environment from as many angles as possible. Then, once you have obtained these shots, you can have your camera and soundman move inside the vehicle to record dialogue. Then, when you edit your film, you will have a complete scene with a high level of production value.

Bad Cameraman, Bad!

Though it is the cameraman who can provide a film with a great look, it is also the cameraman that can ruin a scene and cause you to either have to scrap the scene altogether or to cause you to be forced to re-shoot it. For this reason, it is essential that you maintain control over what your cameraman is doing.

Cameramen, as everyone else in the filmmaking process, have egos. And, just as the egos have been the primary source of problems on a film set, that too is the case with the ego of a cameraman.

I too have been affected by bad cameramen and their egos. For example, when I was filming, *The Final Kiss,* AKA, *Blood on the Guitar,* I had hired a cameraman who had worked with me briefly before. The main reason I hired him is that he had this quick-paced, news cameraman style to his cinematography. And, that is what I wanted for several scenes in that particular film, as it was a dialogue-based film and I thought it would add some flair to all of the talking.

He and his style was fine up until the point when I wanted to add some red gel lighting to a night scene. He was totally opposed to it. But, it was <u>MY</u> film! I was the source of his getting paid! So, believe me, I was going to do what I wanted to do!

After the scene had been lighted, I decided that it would be best, and most expedient, if we shot the scene with two cameras. So, the cameraman shot the scene, as did I. When I looked at his footage, when I began to edit the film, I realized that he had totally blown out the aperture on his camera. He consciously did this so that the lighting would not match what I had filmed at all. And, he had done this on purpose because of the fact that he did not like gel lighting. So, in no way, would what I filmed have matched what he filmed.

Now, due to my style of filmmaking, this did not hold me back from integrating his footage into the final product by adding additional film grain to his footage. But, the moral of this story is, no matter how many credits a cameraman may have or how professional they seem to be, you must never wholly trust them. You must look at all of their camera settings and their screen before you allow them to film a scene, or it may cause you a re-shoot.

Autofocus

Another situation happened to me when I hired a cameraman I had previously worked with on, *Guns of El Chupacabra*. I was filming parts of the U.S. segment of, *Hitman City* on this stage in Hollywood. The action that was taking place was that a police detective was interrogating various suspects. Now, again, this cameraman I hired was a professional with a long list of credits and tons of equipment. I didn't even suspect he didn't know how to use his camera. But, luckily, I too was filming.

What occurred is that deep into the shoot, one of my production assistants came up to me and told me that the cameraman was filming in autofocus mode. Now anybody, who knows anything about cameras, knows that you never use autofocus. Why? Because it always focuses on the central object. In this case, it was a set of prop lockers we had setup behind the main players. So, the lockers were constantly central to frame, as such, they were in focus. But, this left the actors out of focus. This could have killed my movie had I not been using two cameras.

A day or two later, the cameraman called me up asking how everything turned out. I did not call him back, as I was more than annoyed—I had paid him a lot of money. He called again, a week or so later and asked, *"Are you not calling me back because everything turned out badly?"* The answer was, *"Yes."*

This again leads us to the point of—though it is a daunting job, you need to be in control of every aspect of your production. Or, you need to place a person that you can trust, in control of the various aspects of your production. For if you are not in control—if you believe that one of your crewmembers is a professional and, as such, can be trusted, you are opening yourself and your production up to failure. Because, believe me, if it is not their money on the line, no one but you truly cares about your production.

The Good Cameraman

Though it is the cameraman who holds one of the strongest potentials for messing up your production, it is also the cameraman who can give you some great results. A man I have worked with on several of my recent *Zen Films,* Michael Ebert has proven to have great potential to capture what I am seeking. Also, Hae Won Shin, who has worked with me both in the U.S. and Asia, has provided me with great cinematic results.

Ultimately, what you have to do is either find a cameraman who understands what you are looking for and has the potential to actually capture it on film or you have to film it yourself. Filming it yourself is, in fact, what I suggest as the best alternative to hiring a cameraman. Because if you can develop the skills of a highly competent cinematographer, then not only can you film your own movies, but you will know the advanced techniques of cinematography and be able to guide your cameraman into filming what you hope to capture on film.

Cinematic Style

What you ultimately want to do is to assign one cinematic style to your production and keep it fairly constant throughout. I believe we have all seen movies where it starts out fast paced and the camera work is great. Then, all of a sudden, everything just becomes expected and boring, as if some other cinematographer took over. So, whatever cinematic style you assign to your project, try to stay with it. From this, your audience is given a complete package and is not left wondering, *"What happened?"*

This does not mean that the cinematic style of all of your films has to be the same. Though if your want to do that, it is totally up to you. But, what it does mean is if you start out with a specific technique, try to keep it going throughout that production.

For example, when I was making, *Vampire Noir*, I wanted a lot of movement during the dialogue scenes. So, in many of the scenes, while the characters were speaking, I had them either driving or walking. In this way, the audience, whether consciously or subconsciously, were instantly alerted to the fact that something big was going to take place the moment the camera locked off and stopped moving.

I did a similar thing with my film, *The Hard Edge of Hollywood*. As this is a very intense docudrama about the indie film practices of Hollywood and what takes place in the lives of the people who live in that world, I limited my production crew, for most scenes, down to my cameraman, who carried a single camera with an attached Sennheiser microphone. From this, he was allowed to truly study the mood and the actions of the characters.

What you choose for your film's cinematic style is entirely up to you. But, if you want to make your film unique, you will need to think about this in order that it may be discussed and understood by your crew, before you ever go up in production.

Impromptu Production

One of the primary things that I constantly emphasize is that you get a camera; take it with you, and whenever you see an interesting scene or event, shoot it! If you have someone with you, either shoot them walking through the scene or have them shoot you in the scene. From this, you will be able to incorporate this footage into a future film project.

I have done this so many times. In most cases I do not even know what I am going to use the footage for. But, when I am putting a film together or editing one I have already filmed, it dawns on me that the pre-shot footage would work great in the current production and extensively add to the film's production value. So, keep a camera with you!

Chapter 10

The Director

The Director is the artistic heart of a movie. It is the Director that must guide a production towards its artistic end.

A Director's job is twofold. First, the Director must guide the actors of a film in the right direction so that their performances are believable. Secondarily, the Director must create the look of a film—providing it with a unique and definitive artistic definition.

Depending on the cast and crew that are supporting a specific Director, his or her job either becomes very easy or very difficult.

Directing the Actor

Directing your actors is one of the most essential elements to the filmmaking process. For it is you, the Director, who must guide the actors to deliver the style of performance that you feel best depicts the storyline of the film. This being stated, from my long years of experience in the film industry, I can tell you firsthand, you can only get out of an actor what they have to give.

You may ask, *"What does that mean?"* What it means is that each individual has a certain range of emotions, traits, and expressions. Though these attributes can be altered slightly—they will never change very much. For this reason, directing an actor is more about casting the right actor for a role than attempting to get an actor to do something that they are not capable of actualizing.

From a personal perspective, I have seen so many novice Directors attempting to get an actor to deliver a scene in a very specific manner. Yet, no matter how hard the Director tries, it was impossible to achieve. Why? Because the actor has not learned how to isolate and control their emotions to the degree that it would take to express the scene in the way the Director had hoped. Again, this goes back to casting, because the Director should have cast an individual who could perform the role in the way they desired.

This situation, of a Director not getting the desired performance, is one of the primary factors that has truly come to define independent filmmaking and has caused many indie productions to emerge unwatchable. Why? Because time and time again novice Directors attempt to force performances out of actors, but the only outcome of this action is a performance that is not believable. Thus, the film is left unwatchable.

Ultimately, it must be understood that trying to force a performance is simply the wrong way to go about directing an actor.

Anger

What commonly occurs when a novice Director is not getting the performance they want from an actor is that they become unduly agitated. From this, they resort to yelling and screaming. But, this type of behavior alienates their cast. And, this is never the way for a Director to achieve moviemaking success.

One of the amusing things that I have witnessed taking place in the ongoing careers of Directors who resort to this level of behavior is that if they have exhibited this behavior in their early films, they continued forward with it throughout their career. It is based in the same emotion as a child screaming and throwing a tantrum until they get what they want. These Directors do this until someone forces them to stop behaving in such a childish and immature manner, usually with a fist to the face or being fired as the Director of a specific film.

So, it is not only the novice Directors who behave in this fashion. It is also the Directors who have worked in the industry but have never truly come to understand the art of directing an actor.

Directing Mistakes

As previously detailed, one the primary mistakes you can make as a Director is going to a place of anger in order to get your actors to perform their role in a specific manner. This is just wrong!

A person can't do what they can't do. And you, becoming angry and yelling at them is not going to change this one iota.

The second common mistake Directors make is to cast people who are not actors or actresses and then expect them to behave as such.

Now, before we go any further, I must preface the previous statement with the fact that, from my personal perspective, casting non-actors has worked wonderfully for me. I have gotten so many great performances out of people who had never set their mind on the path to becoming an actor. But, what has always worked in my favor when I have cast non-actors is that I have given them a role that allowed them to be them. From this, they have had some fun, they get to see themselves on screen, and the overall production benefited from adding additional character development in the storyline.

But, the adverse to this happens when you try to make a non-actor become a specific character in a film. This is particularly the case when you try to force them to memorize dialogue and then spit it out with any level of proficiency.

As a Director, I was exposed to this situation when I was making the film, *Samurai Johnny Frankenstein.*

A friend was helping me put the film together. He had met a girl at a West Hollywood Coffee House and had become quite infatuated with her. For his play into romance with her, he offered her a role in the film. As I tend to be a very easygoing filmmaker, I agreed to the experiment. The problem is, however, not everyone in Hollywood wants to be an actor or actress. In fact, some do not want to chase that illusive dream at all. This was the case with this girl.

The day came where he had scheduled her to perform her scenes. Me, being a very Zen guy, I allowed her to come on the set and try to perform the role my friend had cast her in. But, she was terrible! I mean really bad! She could not provide any level of performance at all. And, as a Director there was nothing I could do to change this fact. She just didn't have it in her.

My plan, post this experience, was to allow her fall by the wayside. But, my friend became obsessed—feeling that he would lose some level of credibility with her if she were not actually seen in the film. So, he went through hours and days of providing the girl with acting training. He actually wrote out dialogue so that they could practice her role in the film. And then, when he felt she was ready, we scheduled a re-shot for her scenes.

Was she any better? Maybe, a little bit. But, her character in the film remained unconvincing.

Was she a nice person? Yes, she was very nice. And, as a person, I liked her very much. But, that has nothing to do with the outcome of a film.

What I am trying to tell you here is, as a Director; do not try to make someone something that they are not. If you simply let them be who they are, all performances in a film become very believable. But, when an actor is forced to memorize tons of dialogue that they could care less about and then told to deliver said dialogue in a convincing manner, this is when the performances in a film become very contrived. And, this style of contrived and forced performances is immediately noticeable by the audience. Thus, it kills a film.

Casting

As stated, the best thing that you can do as a Director is to cast an actor who *"Acts"* in the manner you desire for any given role. By finding this individual, then your job as a Director becomes very easy. All you have to do is give them the slightest of emotional tune-up when they are expressing a word or a sentence in a manner which you feel is incorrect or would play better on the screen if it was expressed from a slightly different realm of emotion.

The fact of the matter is, a good Director, directs his actors very little, if at all. They just cast the right person for the role and then allow them to EXIST in their role.

The Look

The secondary role of the Director is to guide the film towards its artistic end. What this entails is to provide the film with, *"A Look."*

The look of a film is a very abstract element. I mean, let's face facts; most films look exactly alike.

They have no definitive elements that you can describe that truly make them unique in any manner. This is primarily based upon the fact that most Directors do not care about the overall look or style of a film; they only want to present a story. This is not right or wrong; it is just the fact of filmmaking.

Certainly, we have all seen films that have presented a very unique and stylistic overall look to the presentation. This may have been based in camera technique, the lighting, or the generalized atmosphere of the film.

This being explained, it is you, the Director, who must decide how you want the overall presentation of your film to be viewed. Do you only want to present a story? If so, your job has become much easier. You will only need to arrive on your sets and guide your actors through their performances. If, on the other hand, you want your film to have a specific look, then you will need to take the time and the energy to make that happen. This may mean taking the time to guide your lighting technician to add gels to each of your lights, during every element of a scene. Or, to make sure that your cinematographer is obtaining the right camera angles and performing the proper camera moves as he is filming each scene.

Indie Film Verses Hollywood Production

In the indie film market, the Director is truly the one who guides and maintains control over the overall look of a production. This is not the case with high-budget films, however.

On high-budget film sets, there are so many levels of individualized production, that are brought into play, that it is amazing that anything gets accomplished at all. There is the Production

Designer, the Set Decorator, and the Art Director, just to name a few. These individuals, and their crew, each decide how to depict the various elements of a film's overall look. Though it is oftentimes stated the Director is still in control of the artistic look of a film, more times than not, this is not the case. I have personally known several people who made their mark in indie films, moved up to the *"Bigs,"* but were quickly fired the moment they tried to exercise any artistic control over the film they had been hired to direct.

But, this is the great thing about independent filmmaking. A Director can actually exercise their vision and maintain artistic control over a production. They can give it their own unique signature.

For this reason, as you, the Director, go about setting up your next film; decide how you want it to look. Detail what cinematic image you want to project to your audience. Then, go about creating that look in every aspect of the production. From this, you will emerge as a Director who is associated with a specific and unique style of filmmaking.

Chapter 11

Producing a Movie

Whereas directing a film is about artistic interpretation, producing a film is more about the nuts-and-bolts of getting things done. In the independent cinema, however, these two vocations oftentimes overlap. It is quite often the producer who is also the director and perhaps even the screenwriter. From these overlapping of careers, a filmmaker has the potential to make a truly unique and self-descriptive film creation. But, when these occupations overlap, a filmmaker also has the potential to have everything fall apart.

To begin our study of the position of the producer in independent cinema we must initially view the various positions of a producer and how they affect the outcome of a film.

The Producers:
Executive Producer
Producer
Co-Producer
Associate Producer
Assistant Producer
Line Producer

Executive Producer

The Executive Producer provides the money for a film. Though they are not usually considered to have involvement in the actual creative process or artistic look of a film, due to the fact that they are the money behind a movie, they often have a say as to what the Screenwriters, Producers, and/or Directors are actually doing. It is most commonly the

Executive Producer who will decide to fire a Screenwriter or Director if the film is not coming out the way it was promised or if it is taking a turn in a direction that the Executive Producer does not like. It is also oftentimes the Executive Producer who will have a say if a particular Director is or is not hired to direct a specific feature. As money is the basis of all filmmaking, an Executive producer has a lot of overall control.

Producer

The Producer is the individual who is responsible for making things happen during the process of creating a film. They are the ones who hire the crew, obtain the locations, get the filming permits (if necessary) purchase the production insurance, and oversee the fact that a production is on schedule and going according to plan.

In many productions, a Producer yields much more power than the Director. If they feel the Director is not performing up to appropriate standards they are the ones to sit the Director down and tell them how they must change their behavior and relate to the cast and crew in order to get the film completed.

On the adverse side of this equation, if a film is not on schedule or if not being produced as promised, it the Producer who will feel the wrath of either the Production Company or Executive Producer who has hired them to make sure everything occurred according to plan.

Co-Producer

The Co-Producer is the person who works directly under the Producer. They are commonly the ones who are the go-to person, who makes things happen. Though the Producer may be the one who guides the overall productivity of the Co-Producer, the Co-Producer is more times than not the one who is hands-on in all elements of a films' production.

As the Co-Producer is commonly under the guidance of the Producer, they are normally not the individuals who will experience the wrath of the Executive Producer or the Production Company if a film is going awry. None-the-less, they are more times than not the one who is in actual control of a set.

Associate Producer

In the high-budget film industry an Associate Producer is a person who works for and under the direction of the Producer and Co-Producer. They are the ones who are given an assignment and must see that assignment through to its completion.

In the independent film industry, however, the title, Associate Producer is more commonly given to someone as a mean of saying, *"Thanks,"* to an individual who has provided a shooting location for the film or has helped out in some other nondescript manner. Commonly, when you see the title, Associate Producer in the screen credits of an indie film that person will have probably had nothing to do with the actual production of the film other than to having provided a helpful service.

Assistant Producer

The Assistant Producer is a position that it used primarily in the high-budget film genre. Similar to the Associate Producer this is a person who is hired to provide support and assistance to the Producer, Co-Producer, and Associate Producer.

Line Producer

The Line Producer is a person who is hired to go out on location with the cast and the crew and to make sure that all aspects of a production are going according to plan. The Line-Producer reports directly to the Producer and is the eyes, ears, and power on a set.

Particularly in high-budget films, a Producer will rarely travel to the set. It is the Line Producer who is assigned the job of maintaining Production Company control of the cast and crew.

The Budget

The budget of a film is one of the primary factors that a Producer, at all levels of production, is in the position of controlling. And, the budget is undoubtedly one of the most defining factors for the creation of any cinematic project. The simple truth is, how much money you have to spend on a film directly effects how it will ultimately turn out. This is the job of the producer to take whatever monies that are in the film's cockles and use it to make it look as good as possible.

Now, there are numerous ways to make a small film, with a limited budget, look big. Some of those elements are discussed in this book. But, the ultimate truth is, how much money you have to spend will elementally define your film.

This being said, a lot of money is not the end-all guarantee to making a good film. In fact, in many cases, it is just the opposite. For when people are given a large sum of money to make an independent film, more often than not, that money is spent in all of the wrong places.

As money, and the amount of, is one of the primarily defining factors for a film's quality, it is for this reason that so many people are out there attempting to get money to make a film. As I discussed in the chapter, *Financing Your Film,* people are constantly seeking others to bankroll their movie. As discussed, the reason for this is that people believe that they have some great idea or concept or have some *has-been* actor attached to the project. Then, they promise investors that the film is, *"Guaranteed,"* to make money. The reality of independent filmmaking is, however, very few films ever recover the amount of money that it cost to have them produced.

Whether it has been the Screenwriter, Producer, Director, or a combination of the three, whoever puts up the money for a film is being promised a lot of things that will most probably never come true. And, it is the Producer who is left to thank or to blame for whatever outcome a film ultimately reaches.

Money Debacles

As stated, it is the Producer who must decide how and where to spend the money any film possesses. Many times, however, a film's dollars are all spent in the wrong place. This is especially the case if the money is coming from some outside source because the people who have been given the money did not have to earn it the traditional way and so it is like monopoly money—it is not real.

Many indie film Producers get money and spend it on items that have no true value to film. They buy t-shirts, hats, and jackets, with the film's title on them. They have posters made before the film has even gone up and so on. But, what does this spent money equal? It equals nothing to the overall production value of the finished product.

In fact, many a Producer has wasted all of the film's finances before the cameras ever begin to roll. This is why people are so reluctant to give to a new filmmaker—because they have proven they cannot be trusted.

The second area of misplaced money takes place during production. This occurs when one of the Producers has grandiose ideas about a film and spends money all over the place, obtaining the best locations and the highest end equipment possible. But, using this level of equipment has little true effect on the overall look of the film. In fact, many times a film's budget is completely wasted on this style of behavior, which causes the film to never be completed.

I witnessed this exact situation occur on a film I had been hired to act in, based in Houston, Texas.

The film sounded like a great concept, so when I was contacted by the Producer/Director, I was happy to say, *"Yes,"* to the project. When the film was set to go, they flew me down to Houston and put me up in a hotel right next to the freeway. Man, that place was noisy twenty-four-seven. They also flew in Gunnar Hansen, the actor who played *Leatherface* in the original, *Texas Chainsaw Massacre.* All good...

I watched the problem unfold when the Co-Producer/Cinematographer was the one who took over control of the locations and the equipment. As he was the person based in Houston, he had the knowledge of the area and all of the connections. The Director just paid the bills...

Now, as someone who possessed more than a few filmmaking skills by this point in time, instead of merely hanging out in the hotel, I spent my days getting my hands dirty with the crew before I took on my acting role. While I did, I watched as the *local-yokel* would go into equipment rental shops and rent the most expensive high-end equipment that he could find. I mean he had camera dollies, camera tracks, jibs, and lighting that was more suited to a high-end T.V. show than a low-budget indie film. And, he did this all on the Director's dime. I could not believe it. It got so bad that the Director started making comments about how these rental houses and the hotel we were staying at were not going to accept his credit card very much longer.

Perhaps one of the most explicit events occurred when I was asked to drive the Director's Cadillac to this art village where we were to shoot some scenes—which I did. When I arrived, I was told where to park. I parked the car, got out, and went about helping the crew set up the lights for the next shot. The Director arrived in another car, a bit later, and as we were continuing to set up the scene, we hear, *"BAM."* We looked and a large art piece had fallen onto the Director's car and had smashed in the roof. The art community had no insurance and obviously I felt very bad...

The film never got completed. In fact, a few days into it, the Director asked me to take over and take the footage to L.A. and complete the movie—which I would have been happy to do. The other Producer freaked out at this suggestion, however. So, all of the Director's time, energy, and money equaled nothing. To this day, I feel bad for that man.

But, think how many people have experienced a very similar situation. Somebody, some Producer, gets a hold of a credit card or someone else's money and goes to town. Sure, they may have all kinds of dreams about how the film they hope to make is supposed to come out, but it is never completed. So, it all equals nothing!

As the Producer

As the Producer of a film it is <u>YOU</u> that must make that film happen. Whether it is financed on your money or money from somewhere else, it is <u>YOU</u> that must make that film find its way to completion. If the film is not completed, if you have spent the money on foolishness—it is entirely your fault. There is no one else to blame! For this reason, if you take on the job of producing a movie, you must see it through to completion.

You must learn how to make it happen and you must make it happen!

If you run out of money halfway through production, you must find a new source for funds.

If you take the job, you must make the film a reality. Stop perpetuating the fact that, *"Ninety-nine percent of all filmmakers and their projects are bullshit."* Stop being one of those people that talks and makes promises about completing a movie, never to have produced anything.

If you take the job, see it through to completion, and produce a movie!

Chapter 12
Location, Location, Location

It is a basic fact, the more spectacular the locations you use, while filming your movie, the better your film will look. Plus, spectacular locations cause your finished product to possess higher production value, which makes the viewer of your film believe that you spent a lot of money on your production.

On high-budget films, finding and shooting at spectacular locations is very doable. This is because of the fact that they have the money to spend to rent these locations. On an independent film, however, renting high dollar locations usually isn't in the budget. So, as an indie filmmaker, you need to find other methods of providing your film the high production value of spectacular locations that it deserves.

The Film Permit

The Location Scout for a production is the individual who reads the script and then goes out and finds locations that meet the needs of what is detailed on the written page. Once the Director approves the location, the course is set in motion where a member of the production team contacts the owner, finds out the rate, and then rents the location to be used in the film.

Once these basic parameters have been accomplished, a member of the production team goes to the city or county where the location is situated and obtains, *"A Film Permit."* *A Film Permit* is a document provided to a production company, by a government entity, which states that the production company has met all of the requirements to legally film at a specific location. Though obtaining a *Film Permit* is a common action in the filmmaking process, obtaining one does present several obstacles to the independent filmmaker.

First of all, to obtain a *Film Permit,* you must have *Production Insurance.* A production company obtains *Production Insurance* from one of the various companies that offer this type of insurance. The companies that provide this insurance are constantly changing. You can obtain a current list of these companies from SAG.

Though there is certainly nothing wrong with obtaining *Production Insurance.* In fact, it is necessary to have *Production Insurance* if you want to rent high-end equipment, hire a union actor, or obtain a *Filming Permit.* It also protects your production company from being sued if one of your cast or crew is injured during filming. The problem with obtaining *Production Insurance,* especially for the independent filmmaker, is that it is expensive. Whether you obtain it for a day, a week, or a month, it is very pricey. And, many indie film companies just can't afford it.

It is important to note that in most jurisdictions, it is required that you have a *Film Permit,* even if you are shooting at your own house. So, here is one of the first problems you have to overcome on your road to creating an indie film. How do you shoot without a *Film Permit?*

The Reality

The reality is, you can go and film anywhere you like as long as you don't get caught. If you do get caught, however, this is where you must be very politically correct in your responses to law enforcement. To this end, let's look at this situation a bit more in-depth.

Prior to the terrorist attacks on the World Trade Center on September 11, 2001, most cops would see a small production team filming a scene in a public location and think very little of it. Post, 9/11 however, this all changed. A good example of this occurred on the Santa Monica, California pier a couple of years ago when somebody saw two people of Middle-Eastern descent filming with their video camera on the pier. It was all over the news then about how the police and the FBI were looking for those, *"Person's of Interest."* Later it was revealed that they were found and it turned out to be nothing. If that is not racial profiling, I don't know what is.

But, this is the ideal example of what has taken place in the past few years. I can tell you, from personal experience, it has become much more difficult to film at public locations, without someone calling the police and alerting them to your presence. This being stated, getting out there and filming without a permit is, in many cases, the only way an independent production team is going to add needed production value to their film.

Where to Film

One of the main things I always emphasize is to carry a video camera with you at all times. When you see something interesting happening, you can then immediately film it and make it a part of your movie.

For example, when I was filming, *Samurai Johnny Frankenstein,* we were walking outside of one of the cast member's apartments and a fire truck pulls up with lights flashing, responding to a nearby apartment fire. I got my camera out and had the actors walk across the scene, in front of the fire trucks and firemen, and it added great production value to the film.

When we were filming, *Guns of El Chupacabra* we were on our way out to the El Mirage Dry Lake Bed. As we were driving, we noticed that there had been an accident on the highway and a car had flipped over. I grabbed the 16mm Bolex and went and filmed the car. Then, we had one of the film's characters, a reporter, stand in front of the flipped over car and the fire engine, reporting as if the accident had been caused by a Chupacabra. Both of these situations added tremendous production value to the films.

Though these are very specific situations that you cannot anticipate, if you have a camera with you, you will have the ability to make any similar situation a part of your film.

Going Public

Filming at other locations that will add production value to your film is much more controllable. For example, fairs, festivals, parades, parks, and beaches all can provide your film with an interesting and unique backdrop to your storyline. By filming at these locations, you are also provided with numerous *extras* that will pass in front of your camera lens, adding depth and production value to your film.

Wherever you find yourself, you can use your community's unique surroundings to add to your films quality. As I live in Southern California, I frequently use locations such as the Hollywood Sign and Hollywood Boulevard in my films. Though the people from Los Angeles see these places on a daily basis, they are unique to those who do not live here. And, this is the same about the unique elements of your community. They can all be added to your film's overall presentation.

The other way to make the public, and public locations, part of your film is to just go into establishments and film. For example, when I made, *Dinner and Drinks,* my cast and crew from another film were just hanging out. We decided to go out and have dinner at this old Italian restaurant in the Los Feliz section of Hollywood. I handed my cameraman the camera and the rest is history.

This is similar to what I did in, *Undercover X.* Scenes for this movie were filmed at an old bar on 3rd Street in L.A. In fact, I'm very glad that I filmed there because it had been in existence forever and a year or so after we filmed, *Undercover X,* it closed.

All I did was walk in there with my cast and cameraman and we made a movie. We didn't ask. We didn't tell anybody what we were doing. We just did it. And, from that, it added a great level of realism to the film—something that could not have been obtained if I had tried to talk to the owner about filming in his establishment. All that would have equaled was paying a lot of money to rent the place and hiring a lot of professional *extras* to fill up the bar stools.

If you think that people, who are inadvertently included in your movie, are going to get angry with you once your film is released, this is generally not the case. Most people dream about being a part of Hollywood and you are offering them an opportunity that they never even saw coming.

Is It Legal?

Filmmakers often question if it is legal to shoot signs, buildings, and businesses and then include them in their film. For the most part, yes it is. Why? Because if a building or a business is on a public street, they are considered in, *"The Public Domain."* Which means that anyone can see them, so if you happen to be filming and your camera captures their sign, there is nothing illegal about that.

As far as business owners go, in reality, they are getting free publicity. In fact, I filmed this one scene for, *Hitman City* at a Starbucks in Hong Kong. A year or so after the film came out, the Manager of the Starbucks contacted me and thanked me for using his shop.

Free is the right price. So, just go there and do it! If they ask you to stop filming, stop. It's as easy as that.

EST.

In filmmaking, *"The Establishing Shot"* sets up, for the audience, where a scene is taking place. In a screenplay, this shot is abbreviated as, *"EST."*

When adding locations to your film, setting up your *Establishing Shot* can be done virtually anywhere that will help you add depth to your storyline. For example, your scene may be taking place in an apartment. Though you may actually be filming the dialogue portion of the scene in the dumpy apartment building where you live, you may want your audience to believe that it is taking place in a very high-rent apartment building. To this end, what you will do is to go out, find an apartment building that looks the way you desire, and then film it. When you are editing your film together, what you will do is to initially show the shot of the high-rent apartment building before you cut to the interior of your scene, where the dialogue is taking place.

This style of deceptive establishing takes place in all levels of Hollywood productions. As virtually all A-Level productions are shot on sets, these *Establishing Shots* from around the city are commonly used to provide the audience with a geographic frame of reference for where the characters are located.

If you are low-key about it, you can actually film in front of locations such as police stations, city halls, or museums to add to your film's overall production value. In, *"Hollywood P.D. Undercover,"* I filmed in front of the downtown Los Angles Skid-Row police station with no problems what so ever. For the Zen Documentary, *"Interview,"* we filmed in front of *The Screen Actor's Guild,* when it was located on Hollywood Blvd., and *The Director's Guild of America.*

The main thing to understand, when filming at these high-profile locations, is that you cannot go in there big. You must keep your crew to an absolute minimum and you must keep your actors under control. They cannot be handing out, walking around, talking, and bringing attention to themselves.

More than simply using a building for an *Establishing Shot,* many television and film productions actually shoot their primary scenes in one city, while claiming to be in another. What they will do is to send a Second Unit team to a city where they film all kinds of cityscapes and buildings that can be used for *Establishing Shots.* Then, once the actual production is filmed, they integrate these shots into the completed product, thereby, providing the audience with the belief that the production was actually filmed in a different city than it was.

I have used this technique numerous times. Not only shooting cityscapes and *Establishing Shots* in various geographic reigns of Asia, and then shooting the main story in L.A., but by going out and finding either a rundown or high-end building that ideally describes the setting for where I want a scene to take place.

The technique of utilizing *Establishing Shots* in your movie is very easy. But, most importantly, this style of cinematography truly adds to the overall look and production value of your independent film.

How You Film

In addition to where you film, how you film in the various locations you use can add to the overall look of your movie. For example, I find it a very appealing cinematic technique to have a scene take place while two people are driving down a well-lighted street at night. From this, your audience sees the glow of the lights from the passing businesses. As you are on the move, you are not causing anyone to notice your presence and, thereby, you are alleviating anyone reporting you to the local authorities.

How to Film in Public Places

The main thing to keep in mind when you film in public places is that you want to keep your presence to a minimum. If you go in there with numerous cast and crew members, set up a professional tripod and lights, believe me, you are going to get shut down. But, if you go in with a handheld camera, no lights except maybe a handheld battery powered lamp, and just your essential cast, you can get away with filming a lot of great scenes. Why? Because no one will assume that you are filming a movie.

From a personal perspective, I have filmed all over Los Angeles, Tokyo, Taipei, and Hong Kong. What I have done is to go in with a single handheld camera, a single microphone mounted on the camera and do the scene in as inconspicuous a manner as possible. And, I have never had any problems.

But, these are all large cities. What I have found is that as long as you are low-key in large cities, (except in Seoul, South Korea), the police have far more important things to do than to deal with someone who is not bothering anyone and is simply filming with a digital video camera. This being stated, depending on where you film, you may be accosted by security guards or the police.

When the Police Arrive

It is an inevitable fact of life that if you are filming without a permit, sooner or later, a security guard or the local authorities will contact you. This has happened to me many times. When we were filming, *The Roller Blade Seven,* in the California high desert, a sheriff's helicopter actually flew in. When I was filming, *Samurai Ballet,* the L.A.P.D. drove up and asked what we were doing. When we were filming on the escalators at The Beverly Center, in Beverly Hills, filming, *Samurai Vampire Bikers from Hell,* security asked us to leave. Mind you, this was on the same night that the 1992 L.A. Riots broke out. When I was filming, *Vampire Blvd.* in L.A.'s Chinatown, a security guard asked us to leave. And, these are just a couple of examples. But, when I stack up these few instances against all of the locations I have used, for all of the films I have made, without ever obtaining a filming permit, these few times are minimal.

The main thing to do when you are accosted, (while filming), by a local authority is to be nice. Don't come at them with attitude or they will come back at you with the same and they are in a position of authority. I have known filmmakers who, when the authorities arrived, claimed that they had the right to do what they wanted, wherever they wanted. From this, in each case, they were either heavily fined, their equipment was confiscated, or they were taken to jail.

In most cases, in the large cities, the police just want to make sure that everything is under control and you are not doing anything illegal (other than filming without a permit). Security guards are a little bit more hardcore. I guess due to the fact that they all wish they could be cops. But, they will usually ask you to leave. Just say, *"Sorry,"* pack up and walk away.

Don't Make the Location Essential

This leads us to one of the main points you have to contend with when you film without a permit. You may be kicked out of the location so you do not want to base your entire production around the fact that you must film on a particular site. You must be willing to move to a new location. Or, you must be willing to come back when the guards or police are not around. Both of these situations have happened to me.

I was filming a scene for a movie at Vasquez Rocks and a Park Ranger came up, and very rudely told us to leave. I inquired, wasn't this a Los Angeles County Park? Which it is. But, they would have none of it. They insisted I get a *Film Permit* in downtown Los Angeles. As I was nice, there was no confrontation. So, I just left and went and filmed the remainder of the scene at a different location in the same area.

When we were filming the climactic scene for, *Samurai Johnny Frankenstein* near the railroad tracks in a rundown section of L.A., the Train Cops actually pulled up on a locomotive and told us we had to leave. Now, this was a location where you could see people shooting-up, prostitutes doing their job on their Johns, and they told us to leave! Though I presented this fact to them, they were insistent. What we did was to go and have lunch, then we went back and finished the scene. As this time we knew what to look for, an oncoming slow locomotive...

So, how you actually make filming without a permit work for you is up to you. What I can tell you is that it has worked for me on numerous films. You just have to be cool headed and be ready to change your plans at a moment's notice. Now, this has the potential to affect your cast members, so you either have to know the people you are working with or make sure that any new cast member is cool with this guerilla style of filmmaking.

Never Tell 'em You're Making a Movie

One time, when I was doing a film with Don Jackson, he had discovered this park with a very nice lake in it. He wanted to film some scenes for an upcoming feature that we were going to make. In tow with us that day were a cameraman, an actor and actress who we had worked with before, the man who was going to invest in Don's next film, and two new actresses. We get there, we start to film, and within a few minutes the cops arrive.

This park was in a small community in one of the suburbs of Los Angeles. And, small town cops are always much less forgiving to the independent filmmaker than the aforementioned big city cops.

In any case, Don took the investor and went and hid. This was his *Modus Operandi* whenever cops would arrive, which I always found was a very uncool thing to do. I believe, if it is your movie, you should step-up and take responsibility. But, that was not his M.O.

But, in any case, the cops allowed the actresses to leave. He had the actor, the cameraman, and myself sit down on the ground. He then forcefully asked us what we were doing.

Now, here is a very essential point to keep in mind when shooting without a permit—*NEVER tell them that you are shooting a movie!* Because the minute anyone hears that you are shooting a movie, they think big money, Hollywood production, and the like. And, once they hear, *"Movie,"* there is no way to change your story.

The moment you say that you are shooting a movie, the entire game changes!

For this reason, you can make up whatever story you like. What I generally tell any authority figures that have accosted me, while I am filming, is that I am shooting a, *"Birthday Video."* What is a *Birthday Video?* Hell, if I know? But, neither will they. They will assume that you are not making a movie. And, that is what you want them to think.

In any case, the policeman ran the three of us for warrants and the like. He then wrote down our information and promised to pass it along to the detectives to see if they would like to file charges, as if that would scare us, or something…

The funny thing that occurred, just as he was saying this to us, there was a couple in their wedding outfits, being videotaped over by a fountain which

128

sprouted out of the lake. I inquired as to why they were not being questioned and told to stop filming. He had no answer.

The main point of this story is that the moment all of this melodrama was completed, our two new actresses were completely freaked out and had already called a cab to take them back to our office, where they had left their cars. I went up to them and told them that we would be happy to take them back, after we went to this other, very grandiose, location that we had filmed several movies at, but they declined. They wanted out of there… Well, at least they didn't stall our production, and they paid for their own cab fare home…

Each independent filmmaker will ultimately have their own stories to tell about the various locations that they either tried to use or succeeded in using in the creation of their feature film. The main thing to remember is that as an indie filmmaker, you do not possess the financial resources of a high-budget production. So, if you want to get your movie made, you will have to cut corners to make it happen.

At the end of the day, all that matters is that you <u>DID</u> get your movie made. And, if you can make it look as <u>BIG</u> as possible, by using as many interesting locations as possible, then you will have added to the overall quality of your film while not decreasing from your bank account.

In closing, what you will want to do when defining the locations for your independent feature film is that you will want to locate all of your main dialogue scenes in a location that you have total control over; be it your house, your apartment, a friend's house or apartment, or a business where they will let you shoot uninterrupted. A location where your production can be locked-down and not disturbed. Then, you will want to find as many unique locations in your area as you can and then bring your cast and crew out to them and shoot these locations to the best of your ability; knowing that if you get shut-down you will just move along as you have not based your entire production around filming at one of these unsecured locations.

Chapter 13

The Two-Day Movie

When I tell people that they should film their independent movies in two days, they most often respond, _"That's impossible!"_ But, I can tell you from personal experience, that, _"No, it is not."_ In fact, I have made an art out of shooting entire feature films in just two days.

This process began when I made, _Samurai Vampire Bikers from Hell._ Making a film this quickly was in direct response to the months-upon-months Don Jackson and I took to make, _The Roller Blade Seven._

While making _RB7_ I came to the realization that though all of the time we had spent during production had, for the most part, been a fun experience, it truly did not make the movie any better.

Now, _RB7_ was filmed in numerous locations—many of which were a long distance from our offices on Hollywood Boulevard. The truth being told, if you are going to shoot at that many locations, with that much of a distance to travel, then, _"No,"_ you probably cannot make your movie in two days. But, if you keep your locations central to your homebase, then this style of filmmaking is very doable.

Why

The question is often posed to me, _"Why make a film in only two days."_ The logic is simple. First of all, it is cheaper. If you are paying or feeding anyone on your set, then keeping the shooting schedule limited to only two days cuts way down on your production costs. Secondarily, and perhaps most importantly, people have lives, people have jobs, people have families, people have egos that can be damaged, people have the belief that your production is not that great, and they will soon be offered a bigger position in a larger production. In short, your crew and particularly your cast are going to move on. But, if you shoot your film in a minimal period of time, their interest will remain high, and they will stay onboard until the completion of your production.

In addition, the two-day film really works great for the working masses, because you can make an entire film over the weekend. As most people work Monday thru Friday, their weekends are open. With this, they do not feel that they are being cheated out of their daily wage for taking part in your production.

Also, if you need to rent equipment, film rental houses have a policy that renting equipment for the weekend is billed as a single day rental. So, if you need to rent equipment, you can save some money.

Scheduling

The successful two-day film is all about scheduling. Whereas many novice indie filmmakers go into their project with their script in hand and the idea of what they hope to film on a particular day, their schedule quickly becomes lost due to the fact that they are messing around with the lights, talking and joking with the cast, rehearsing their actors, and generally not getting anything done. If you are going to make a two-day movie, you need to know how to get things done!

On every film, there are things that are going to come up that you cannot anticipate, and these situations will lead to your planned schedule being altered to some degree. So, what you want to do is to alleviate as many of those potential problems as possible. For example, you will want to <u>KNOW</u> your locations.

With the two-day movie you cannot just show up to a place you have never been to before and expect everything to go fine. Maybe everything will go fine, but that cannot be guaranteed.

So, when planning for the two-day movie, prior to shooting, you will want to visit, dress the sets, and setup your lights, if possible, at each location to fit the needs of your film. Then, on the day of shooting when you travel to the location it will be ready to go.

Scheduling the Actor

One of the primary things that you will want to do, particularly in regard to actor scheduling, is to only bring them onto the set when it is near the time for them to shoot their scenes. So many filmmakers bring actors onto the set and then have them sit around for hours, if not all day. Sometimes these actors are not even used if a filmmaker encounters any problems. This is just the wrong way to make the independent film.

What this style of filmmaking does is to alienate your actors from you and the production and cause them to be discontent. By the time you are ready to shoot their scenes—if, in fact, you ever get around to them, their emotions are displaced and they are not happy—which may be projected into your film. So, the main thing you have to do is to decide the order of the scenes you are shooting on a specific day, in a specific location, and then bring the actors onto the set near the time you plan to begin shooting the scenes that involve their character.

There will certainly be lead or co-star actors and actresses that will need to travel with you to the various locations you are shooting at on a given day. What I find works best is to meet them at the first location, if this location is some distance from your primary set. Shoot their scenes at this location and then move onto the next set or location. You can either have them leave their car at this location or have them follow you.

The other thing to do is to meet at your primary set and then drive in one car with them. With this style of transportation, not only can you discuss any questions they have about their character or the scenes you are going to shoot, but you can also learn about their personality. From this, you, as a director, will better know how to guide them through their performances.

The main thing you do not want to do is to lose you actors in the process of the two-day movie. Because, with no cast, there is no character development, and your movie can never be completed—at least not as scheduled. So, you want to keep your lead actors close.

The Look

The two-day film does not have to look low-budget. With a schedule of ten to twelve hours a day, you can shoot a lot of character development at a lot of locations and give your film the look of a production that took much longer to create and cost much more. Achieving this is easy. Chart out your locations, film your scenes at them and then move on to the next location. Don't mess around. You can do that later. Get out there and get your movie filmed.

Those Who Get It

Let's face facts, some people, *"Get it,"* and some do not. Some understand that an indie film is a low-budget collaborative process that is designed to be a stepping-stone process to make inroads in the film industry and some do not. What you want to do when making the two-day film and, in fact, when making any indie film, is surround yourself with a cast and crew that *"Get it."* From this, you will alleviate many of the problems that may occur, particularly with your cast.

The Reality

The reality of the two-day movie is that you can create a very nice product while interfering with the lives of your cast and crew in the most minimal manner possible. With this, they come away with a new credit on their resume while having had a positive experience.

If, while editing you find that you need another scene or two to fix any holes in the story, as the production was so trouble free your cast and crew will be happy to come back and give you another hour or two.

The problem with long independent productions is obvious. The cast and the crew become too involved in the lives of each other, and from this, the flaws in the production and individual personalities are revealed. This abrasive reality drives many people away. From this, the film can never be completed in the manner in which it was hoped. The solution; the two-day movie. You get in there, you get it done, and everyone moves on with his or her life.

Chapter 14
You Get What You Pay For

The reality of making an independent feature film is that you get what you pay for. Indie films are not high-budget Hollywood productions. They are a unique subculture onto themselves. Thus, they should not be judged in comparison to a high-budget feature film. Yet, that is exactly what everyone does.

The budget of an indie film is anywhere from $1.00 on up. But, the truth of the matter is, no matter how much money you spend, your indie production will never look like a studio feature film.

The Reality

People who enter into the world of indie filmmaking do so for many reasons. The prevailing motivation is that <u>ANYBODY</u> can make an indie film. You do not have to be rich, born into Hollywood royalty, or educated at the finest schools of filmmaking. You can simply be a guy or girl with a video camera who is ready to get out there and get your hands dirty.

Though anybody can make an indie film, many who do so are very dissatisfied with the end result. This goes for both the filmmakers and the actors who take part in the production. Why is this? Because these low-budget indie features do not come out looking like a high-budget studio film. The fact of the matter is; people expect more than what can be delivered on a limited budget, which is what indie films have.

One of the primary causes for the mindset of intermingling studio and indie films is the fact that there are a lot of films out there that are presented to people, particularly people in the industry, as, *"Independent."* Though in theory they may be, in fact, *Independent,* they were made with a very high-budget. I have seen *Shorts* that were billed as *Independent* but they cost over five million dollars to create.

When filmmakers and actors are exposed to this level of production and told that it is *Independent,* they come to believe that all independent productions will come out with that level of production value. But, this is not the case.

A guy with his video camera, even if he does light his scenes very well, will not be able to produce a product that possesses the production value of a feature that was created by highly professional and experienced crewmembers, using top of the line cameras, lighting, and audio equipment. Thus, most people are let down.

In reality, most filmmakers and actors have never seen a truly independent film. A film that was made with a shoestring budget by a cast and crew that have worked for free with the sole intent of making a small film look as good as it can look.

Throwing in the Towel
The intermingling of film labels, reality and non-reality, has been the basis for many an indie filmmaker to throw in the towel even before the film was completed. They look at the footage, see the flaws when it is compared to a high-budget production, become very disappointed, and shut down their production. From this, everybody involved has wasted his or her time, energy, and money.

As an indie filmmaker, what your film has the true potential to actually come out looking like is a fact of life that you must take into consideration before you ever bring up a production. You must accept the fact that your film will never look like the blockbuster feature you saw at the movie theatre last weekend.

Many novice indie filmmakers think that this is not a problem. They believe that they are very talented and they can make anything look good. Maybe… But most do not even consider the fact of production let down until they view their footage.

The main thing to know is that if you do not prepare yourself for the probable end results you will be let down.

The Edit

One of the sad but true realities of indie filmmaking is that the resolution and image quality on a computer screen is far different than that of a television screen—even if the T.V. screen is high def. What commonly occurs is that some footage will be shot and then uploaded to a computer to be edited. Once the edit is complete and the footage is output, to whatever media is used, it is then played on a television set. The filmmaker then cannot believe what he or she is seeing. *"It looks so much like video,"* is the common exclamation that is made. *"It didn't look that way on my computer!"*

Here again we meet a simple reality of the game, and a factor that must be taken into consideration before you ever bring up a production—video is video.

The Early Days

I was one of the first filmmakers to make a feature film on video, (Hi-8 to be exact), which received international distribution. So, I felt that I played a small part in the overall evolution of the video filmmaking revolution. But, even today in the western world, people are addicted to the look of film.

In Asia, Europe, and South America, this is not so much the case. This is due to the fact that they have been more exposed to video production running throughout their media. In the west, however, this is not the case.

For this reason, since the dawning of the video age, there has been processes utilized that have attempted to make video look more like film. The, *"Film Look"* process is perhaps the most notable.

But, video is still video. Due to this fact, even though many of the high-budget features are now filmed using video equipment, the cameras utilized are virtually nothing like the prosumer cameras that the indie filmmaker uses. Plus, the process that the filmed video footage goes through before it is ever shown to the audience is also vastly different from anything that an indie filmmaker has at his or her disposal.

The main point is, *Your film is not going to come out looking like a high-budget Hollywood production!*

This being stated, that does not mean that you cannot take the time to make your production look as good as it possibly can look. You can light it properly. You can use good microphones, so you obtain good audio. And, you can employ good camera techniques. But, you must accept the fact, and prepare your cast for the realization, that your film is going to look like it looks.

I do not know how else to tell you this. But, do not expect high-budget results from a low-budget production or you will be very disappointed.

I have seen so many people go out and buy expensive cameras only to be so disappointed in what these cameras are capable of producing that they put them and their filmmaking ideas away and never again attempt to pursue the craft of filmmaking.

From the opposite perspective, I have also seen people, with no money and little experience, go out and produce some great, very artistic, and very watchable indie features. So, it can be done. Are you the one to do it remains the only question?

_____*Chapter* 15

Who's in Charge?

On large film productions the hierarchy of a film crew and the expected task of each crewmember is highly defined. This is primarily due to the fact that each person is hired and, as such, if they do a poor job they will be fired. For this reason the majority of people who come onto a high-budget set do their job to the best of their ability and leave their ego in check.

On a high-budget set you will often see more crewmembers than you can count. Some of them are working while others are sitting around waiting to be told what task it is they are expected to do next. Whatever task that is—it is ultimately a part of their specific job and they have done it numerous times before.

On a high-budget set, jobs rarely overlap. Rarely will you ever see a grip, for example, helping a lighting technician rig the lighting for the scene or an actor helping the soundman with a boom poll.

This is not the case with an independent film, however. In fact, it is very common that actors and crew alike work on every part of a film's production. Though this can be a great experience for all involved, this mindset can also cause a person's roll in the production to become convoluted. From this, egos come into play and people try to exert their control in areas where they should not, and this can negatively affect a production.

What's Your Job?

An example of this happened to me early into my emersion in the film industry—when I was creating one of my first feature films, *Samurai Johnny Frankenstein*. I had invited this guy to come onboard and help me produce the movie. On this particular day, we had several cast and crewmembers at our downtown Los Angeles location.

Now, it must be understood, on a film set, there can be only one, *Captain of the Ship*. Though you have people helping you on many levels, there can be only one guiding force or a project becomes convoluted.

On this day, the shooting was progressing and we had planned to meet up with this one actress that my associate was infatuated with and wanted to put in the movie. Though I was happy to have her in the film, I had a realization that due to time and location constraints, we should wait until the next day to use her because I realized that we could shoot her character's scenes at a much better location. I explained this to him and he completely freaked out. He started yelling and screaming—which ultimately upset my cast.

One has to question, where does this kind of reaction come from—because most people would not react like this. They would understand and readjust their thinking. But, in film production, the common factor of an individual's involvement is, *"Ego."* People in the film industry believe that they are important, special, have something to offer, and their opinion should matter above all others.

Though I put this situation to rest fairly quickly. And, ultimately, the man realized that my choice of shooting the girl at a different location was, in fact, the best thing to do for the overall production value of the film. But, the damage this type of behavior can unleash upon a production may never be repaired.

I have seen this style of behavior on many independent film productions. It is usually unleashed by those at the top of the totem pole of the production; i.e.: the Producers, the Directors, or the Stars. In each case, it does nothing to help the production. And, in fact, hurts it.

From this style of combative behavior I have seen both actors and crew walk off of a set. From this, the production is left waiting to fill the position of the person who left. Thus, some of these productions have actually shut down, never to be completed. Thus, the money, the time, and the energy to bring that production up where all lost.

Hotdogs

A curious situation happened when Donald G. Jackson and I were filming, *Armageddon Boulevard.* He and I were both very busy on the set. We were shooting on this small stage that we frequently used in Hollywood. The cast, and most prominently Don, had become hungry. Personally, I never eat while I'm filming as I feel it brings down my energy. In any case, there was this one co-star not doing anything in particular but sweet-talking the actresses, so Don asked if he would head over to Pink's and pick everybody up some hotdogs. I mean we were paying for them... He agreed, though he could have easily said, *"No,"* and we would have just asked somebody else. When he came back, he was in a huff, however, as I guess his ego had come into play. He walked back onto the stage angry. *"You know, I wear Armani suits,"* he proclaimed as he threw the hotdogs down on a table. All this was-what-it-was, but in the process of picking up the hotdogs, he had put something on Don's, which ultimately made him very sick. I guess he blamed him. Me, as I never eat on the set, was fine. Don went home. I continued on with the production.

This situation details how you, as a filmmaker, must be very careful about the people you bring onto your set and what you ask people to do. As an actor, the previously described guy was great. As a Production Assistant, however, his actions speak for themselves.

The main thing to know is that this style of behavior is prevalent throughout all levels of production. Though it may not be so demonstrative as the previously described situation. Or, in fact, it may be worse. The main thing to understand is that ego is everywhere on a film's production. What you, as a filmmaker, and the *Captain of the Ship* must do is to learn how to gage the behavior capacity of each of your individual cast and crewmembers and know that everybody has an ego and a breaking point. So, what you want to do is to keep random and undisclosed assignments and requests to a minimal, in order that you let your cast and your crew feel that they are the stars of the production—as long as they do not step over any lines, let them bask in their ego and glory. Because the reality of the filmmaking game is, the production that they are currently working on may be the last job they ever get.

The Producer

More than solely babysitting your cast and crew, it must be understood that Producers are the most notorious for attempting to take control over a production and guide it in a direction that it was not originally intended. They are also the ones who possess the power and the ability to truly derail a film's ultimate outcome.

For example, a friend of mine was directing a 16mm production that had a budget of about $100,000.00. He had been hired to Write and Direct the film. The Executive Producer then hired a Producer to keep the project on schedule. The problem was, the Producer wanted to be the Director of the film so he continued to disrupt the sets by being rude to the cast and crew and frequently reported back to the Executive Producer that the Director was doing a terrible job.

This is the problem when people are hired for an indie film. Though they may be getting paid, it is probably not that much, so it would not be life-altering if they were fired. Furthermore, people view indie films as a pathway to gaining employment in higher budget productions. For this reason, there is a lot of cut-throat activity that have the potential to manifest on an indie set—particularly when it is a higher-budget indie set as the one just described.

Ultimately, due to the fact that my friend own the rights to the characters in the film and wrote the script, he won out. But, this did not stop many of the cast and crewmembers to come to view this as a completely miserable set. And, why was this? Because the Producer tried to exercise his power to climb up the Hollywood ladder.

When Things Go Wrong

Now, this previously described Producer was busy exercising his power only because the production was going according to plan. And, this was also the case with the previously described situations. But, *"Going According to Plan," is* not always the case on a filmmaking set. Let's face facts;

things go haywire sometimes. And, you can never predict when this may occur. In this situation, it is never the ego-filled cast or crewmember that steps up to the plate and tries to fix what went wrong. They only stand around with dumb looks on their faces and wait for you to decide what to do.

This is an essential element to filmmaking that you must take into consideration whenever you bring up a production. It is going to be you that will ultimately have to fix anything that is broken. So, as previously detailed, people help you on many levels when you are making an independent film. But, at the end of the day, there is only one person who is responsible for what takes place, when things go wrong. More times than not, they are not going to be the ones to fix what is broken.

Just a Moment That Passes in Time

From a personal experience, when I was making one of my first feature films, *"Just a Moment That Passes in Time,"* my manager at the time, was the one to suggest that I write and direct a film. She was the one who was going to put it all together and produce it—so she claimed.

Previous to this, I had shot several documentaries in Asia and the U.S. Plus, I had acted in many productions, so I was not alien to the game, on any level. But, I was new to theatrical production. So, as she had been in the industry forever, I allowed her to take control. She had cast the film, had secured a few locations, and had gotten a crew. We were up.

Initially, everything went okay. The actors did their scenes. The crew shot the footage.

The problems began to emerge, however, from whom she had cast. The first, somewhat amusing, occurrence happened when the attractive

Middle-Eastern girl she had cast as the female lead, had apparently not read the script. There was a scene where she kissed my character goodbye. The problem was, being a good Muslim girl; she had literally never kissed anyone before. My Manager/Producer had a talk with her and the scene went forward. Though in viewing it, the scene played very strained—for obvious reasons. So much for a first kiss…

Then, came the outdoors scenes where the martial arts were to take place. The minute I began to set up the first scene I realized that all of the people she had cast had absolutely no martial arts experience. I guess she just assumed anyone could do a jumping spinning heel kick?

So, beside myself, there was no one on the set who could actually do anything. Though I had trusted her to cast people with martial arts experience.

I believe it was due to the fact that she began to see her own folly that she then began to present all of these unrealistic ideas. For example, she suggested that I have actors jump off of a roof and into the scene. Now, this would have all been great, if she had planned for it. But, without the proper fall-padding, this could not safely happen.

It is in these moments, when things begin to go haywire, that you, as a filmmaker, truly begin to see that people do not really care about your production and are only in it for themselves—for whatever reason. You witness that instead of them stepping up and trying to remedy any problem, they sidestep their involvement by doing all kinds of non-essential activities such as making unrealistic production suggestions.

Perhaps the most amusing thing on this set occurred as I was attempting to choreograph the actors to make their fighting look even plausibly real. During this process, a well-known actor of the time, (he had his own T.V. show), saw cameras and drove up to see what was going on. For me, not being enamored with stardom on any level, this was nothing but a distraction. But, for the rest of the cast and crewmembers, they were quite star-struck and the production pretty much skidded to a halt. In fact, my manger was so enthralled, trying to get the man to sign her as his Manager, that she was not even paying attention to the fact that we were losing the light. So, again, it was one central filmmaker, me in this case, that had to pull the gawking eyes back together and get the movie filmed.

Who's In Charge?

This brings us to the main point of this chapter. Independent productions are not high-budget productions. There are not more people than you need on the set to fulfill each occupation. Therefore, though you may hire a cameraman, a soundman, a makeup artist, a gaffer, or lighting technician, the job they are brought on to do, may not end up being their only job. In fact, they may do their required job so poorly that you or someone else must take over their job in order to see a production through to its completion. This is true for above-the-line crewmembers such as the Director and the Producers, as well. Each person on an independent film may end up doing all kinds of things. And, this is where the problems begin—because there becomes a lack of definition.

The simple reality of this situation is that you MUST define what each person will be doing before your production actually goes up. This is especially the case with the above-the-line crew. Once the definitions are in place, though they may turn to your crew for suggestions, they should never feel that they have the ability to make them without asking you first.

Let people do what they do. Let them do their specified job. And you, at the top of the heap must act like you deserve to be there. If a problem occurs, step up and try to fix it.

Take control. Be in control. Be the boss.

Chapter 16

Distribution

Distribution is at the heart of getting your film viewed by other people. And, depending on the style of distribution, it is the way a filmmaker gets paid for making a film.

In Times Gone Past

In times gone past, a filmmaker would complete a film and then be paid an upfront fee by a distribution company, in order that they may attempt to sell the film at the various film markets across the globe to the distributors who actually release the film to the various theatrical, television, and video distribution channels in their country. The distribution companies did this because they had learned through experience that they could anticipate making a certain amount for each film they handled. Though these companies assuredly made more money than the individual filmmaker, none-the-less, the filmmaker at least made something by obtaining upfront payment.

Though this is how things were handled in the long-ago and the far-far-away, this is no longer the case. With the dawning of the digital revolution, everybody became a filmmaker and the distributors and the film markets were flooded with filmmakers who each believed that they had created the next great film sensations. With this, upfront distribution fees went out the window and filmmakers had to beg to get a distributor to even handle their film. And, if they did get a distributor, the filmmaker never made any money because the distribution company would write off all sales as distribution expenses. So, a filmmaker basically gave their film away.

The previous reality was, once a distribution company got a hold of a master copy of a film, they would sell it to who knows how many countries via an untold number of distribution channels and the filmmaker would never receive any compensation. For example, my friend Don Jackson's film, *"Demon Lover"* played throughout the country at Drive-In theatres during the 1970s and then it was widely distributed on video during the 1980s and he never received a dime. Plus, I cannot tell you how many filmmakers I have known who have made a feature film, given it to a distribution company, saw the film on Cable T.V. and available via video outlets across the U.S., and also never made a nickel. This was just the name of the game. If you gave your film to a distributor you would probably never make any money from its distribution.

Distribution Today

The event that took place, hand-in-hand with the digital revolution was that of the internet. From this, no longer was a filmmaker bound to a single distribution company who would take their film, sell it, and leave the filmmaker with no way of knowing the exact outcome of any form of distribution. Thus, the filmmaker would make no money.

Now, times have changed. Today, an independent filmmaker can personally take control over their film's distribution. A filmmaker can screen his movie on sites such as *YouTube* or *MySpace*, just to name a few, and develop an audience for it. In addition to these free sites, there are numerous cable television stations all across the country that have nothing but unscheduled time on their hands. All you have to do is to contact them and tell them that you have a film, and they would love to show it. From this, though you generally make no money, your filmmaking style is provided with an incalculable source of free publicity.

Once these sources have been developed, you can sell your film either via your own website or give it to one of the companies that provide POD, *"Print on Demand"* services and sell it via these companies that reach all parts of the globe. By contracting one of these companies to distribute your movie, you will receive approximately fifty percent of each sale. If your movie sells well, you can make a substantial chunk of change from this style of independent distribution.

The Downside

When home-viewing trends evolved from watching videotapes to DVDs, a situation occurred that was not a problem in the past. The problem is, when a person obtains a DVD, what do they have? They have a master quality copy of your movie. This was not the case with videotapes. For anyone who has attempted to make a copy of videotape understands, with each generation the tape gets more and more grainy. DVDs do not have this problem. You can make a million copies and they all remain pristine. Though there is some anti-piracy duplication processes out there, anyone with basic computer lacking skills can bypass these measures. So, people can easily obtain a master copy of your movie.

For the most part, this is not a big problem for the independent feature film. Yes, there may be a few people making copies of your film on their computer and passing them around to their friends, but if there is any buzz going around for your film, your overall sales will nicely compensate for this.

The problem is a little larger for a film that has received more of a worldwide interest. In these cases, if you are traveling the globe, you may see your film being sold in a video shop in some city in Asia. I have…

What can you do? There is really nothing you can do. The video shop owner in Bangkok didn't steal your movie. They simply bought it from someone else who stole it and sold it to them. So, going into a shop and raising a fuss will equal nothing. Just be glad that someone liked your movie enough to make a bootleg copy of it, which ultimately helped in getting your name out there, which may equal interest in your next film.

If, on the other hand, you find someone in the western world selling unauthorized copies of your film, either online or in a store, contact the FBI. Don't mess around threatening to sue them. Instead, get the authorities involved and get it stopped.

The End Result
Ultimately, you have to be philosophical about the distribution of your film in this digital age. First of all, give up the belief that you are going to make a lot of money on a film you shot on a home camcorder. If you do, Great! But, don't expect it. Make any movie for the love of the craft. See every film you make as a steppingstone, learning process that allows you to become a better filmmaker.

Finally, instead of seeking distribution for your film, distribute it yourself. From this, not only do you maintain control over the distribution, but you will also be able to see where your film is selling. From this, you may be able to isolate a specific pocket of interest for your filmmaking style and thereby go to that geographic location, learn what they like about your film, and use that as a marketing tool.

Ultimately, by distributing your film yourself; you maintain a completely independent approach to the entire filmmaking process. With less cooks in the kitchen, you will maintain complete creative control. From this style of distribution, if your film catches on, then the high-end distribution companies will contact you and then you can, *name your own price.*

Chapter 17

Let's Get Legal

The reality of it is, we live in a very litigious society. People are constantly filing lawsuits and threatening to file lawsuits. This is particularly the case with the creative arts—because people are very possessive of what they have created, what they feel they had a hand in creating, and their personal image.

I am not a lawyer, so I am not going to give you all of the specifics of the various legal actions that can take place with you and against you in the world of filmmaking. What I am going to tell you is that you must protect yourself, to the best of your ability, to keep yourself free from lawsuits. Because, at the end of the day, no one truly wins when a lawsuit is filed. And, the only ones who get rich are the attorneys.

A couple of things I can tell is that a lawsuit is fairly easy to file. They are much more difficult to win, however. And, if you do win, it is almost impossible to collect any monies as people or the companies you are suing generally disappear from the face of the globe or file bankruptcy.

Before Filing

Before you file a lawsuit, you have to ask yourself, *"How have you been damaged?"* Why? Because this is what the attorney for the defense and the judge will ask you. Then, you must answer, *"How were the actions of the other person going to damage the future of your career?"* Then, you will need to answer, *"Can you put a specific financial number on how their actions have damaged you?"*

And, you cannot just grab a number out of thin air like twenty million dollars and say, *"That is how much!"* You have to have substantiating proof of how this amount is a valid figure. Finally, you need to decide if suing a person or company is worth spending thousands of dollars and the next several years in court, while the Production Company or the individual you are suing continues to make money on whatever film or performance you are suing them over.

The reality is, most attorneys are not going to be this honest with you. Instead, they will take your money, make you promises, and keep charging you by the hour. Ultimately, what will you gain?

Now, I am not saying that you may not feel faulted and whatever a person did to you was right. But, you will find in all aspects of film production that people only look out for themselves. And, they will lie, cheat, and do whatever it takes to claw their way to the top of the heap. What you have to do is, first of all, not allow yourself to become part of this negative process and do not take actions that negatively affect other people. Secondarily, you need to protect yourself from the ego-based legal actions of others and get the appropriate releases signed and move forward with your production in the most conscious manner possible.

Dissatisfaction

At the end of the day, you have to understand that not everyone who helped you with the film is going to like the finished product. Depending on how nice you were to your cast and crew, they will voice this dissatisfaction in many different ways. But, what you can do is protect yourself by having people sign the appropriate *Release* before you ever use their writing, music, production skills, or acting performances in your film. In this way, you protect yourself from unnecessary legal action.

Though it must also be stated that every contract is open for interpretation and just because a person has a signed a *Release* does not mean that if they have the passion and the finances that they will not sue you for whatever reason they feel they have been violated. None-the-less, by having every person on your cast and crew sign a release, you may help protect yourself from frivolous lawsuits.

Note: you can find various versions of Performer, Screenwriter, Music, and Producer Releases online by searching for them. Simply look through your various choices and then refine the wording of the pre-created forms to match your needs.

Payment

In all *Releases* you must clearly detail that you are either going to compensate a person for their contribution to your film by paying them a specific day-to-day amount, an amount paid for their overall participation for the entire project, or in screen credit only. In many, if not most, independent films, the cast and crew are paid in screen credit only.

The main thing I would suggest steering away from is offering a participant either a deferred payment that is to be made when the film reaches completion or distribution or a percentage of the film's ultimate gross. The reason for this is twofold.

First of all, if you offer to pay a person deferred payment, they will constantly be contacting you for that deferred payment. *"Isn't the film done yet?"* The reality of independent filmmaking is that by the end of production you, the filmmaker, will probably be out of money, as such that is the wrong time to have anyone be asking you to get paid. And, as detailed in the chapter on distribution, if your film does reach distribution, you will most likely not have made any money from it. So, again, this is the wrong time to be asking to get paid.

If you have not offered deferred payment, then your actors will be happy to have received a copy of the completed film. Thus, they will not harass you.

Another common mistake independent filmmakers make is to offer Screenwriters and Producers a percentage of the film once it is sold or in distribution. Again, as previously stated, just because a film has received distribution does not mean that you have made a dime. Or, maybe you have just made a dime and nothing else. As the primary filmmaker, you will want and need to keep that money to move forward onto your next project. If you have signed a contract with someone promising them a percentage, at any time they can force you to open your books. And, this is to no one's advantage.

I have found that the best thing to do is to make your cast and crew happy and proud just to be a part of the film. If you are going to pay them, do so, whatever amount you have decided upon, at the end of each day of shooting. From this, no matter what their pay scale is, from free on up, each person will have felt that they have gained something just by becoming a part of your production.

Action-Packed

Finally, many independent films have various forms of action in them; be these martial arts, weapons, car chases, foot chases, and various stunts. In the *Performer Release* you use, it must be stated that the actor will not hold you liable if they get hurt. Though this clause is virtually meaningless, as you cannot sign away your rights in the United States of America or most other countries for that matter. It does, however, provide you and any judge who views the documents with the fact that your actor did anticipate getting hurt and they consciously released you from liability. So, it may help.

This being stated, be careful. Don't have people do things where they can and possibly will get hurt. If you are having stunts performed in your movie, get professional stunt people and have people on the set who know how to choreograph and rig these stunts. But mostly, if you are going to create this style of film, have production insurance because if somebody gets hurt, you do not want them to halt the creation of your production, and you most certainly do not want them to sue you.

My main advice is to be nice to your cast and crew. A person who likes you will be much more forgiving than the person who feels they have been treated badly or without respect. And, as stated previously in this book, tell people what to expect when they come onto your set. From this, they will not have dashed the cast member's unrealistic expectations, and they will come to appreciate that you are offering them a stepping-stone opportunity to learn by being a part of an independent film.

Conclusion

The ultimate fact about independent filmmaking is that it is a process of trial and error. You shoot a scene, then you study it, find your mistakes, and the next scene you film will be better. You make a movie, you study it, and your next film will be improved. It is as simple as that. Though your first shooting experience may have moments of genius in it, there will most likely be scenes you hate or cannot use at all. This is the nature of the game.

This process of trial and error is perhaps the greatest element in the craft of independent filmmaking, in that it provides you with the opportunity to learn from your mistakes. As most independent filmmakers begin by financing their own early projects, there is no one you will have to pay back. So, you can take some time, film some scenes, make some movies, and hone your craft.

The primary message I always like to pass onto new filmmakers is that there are no longer any rules or definitions that a filmmaker, particularly an independent filmmaker, must adhere to. With the dawning of the digital age, and all of the creative techniques that occurred hand-in-hand with this era, you can do anything. Everything can be considered art. With this as a basis for formulating your filmmaking plans, you can get out there and do it. Make a film the way you want to make it.

Today, filmmaking has become relatively cheap. So, if you want to be a filmmaker, be a filmmaker! Get out there and make a movie!

Fast Facts
for the Independent Filmmaker

1. Always carry a camera with you.

    When you see an interesting situation or scene, film it for use in a later film.

2. Always put a UV filter on your camera lens.

    Camera lenses are easily scratched or damaged. If you damage your lens, your lens or your entire camera can be ruined. A UV filter is cheap, replaceable, and protects your lens.

3. Always close the latches on your equipment cases.

    If your case is not locked, one of your crewmembers or yourself may pick it up, allowing all of the contents to fall on the ground and be damaged or broken.

4. Always carry Performer Releases with you.

    By doing this, if you see an interesting person you want to integrate into your film, you will be allowed to use their performance once they sign the release.

5. Tell your crew and especially your cast exactly what to expect on your set.

    Never exaggerate about your production simply to get someone to come onto your set, because they will be disappointed and may leave.

6. Always provide your cast and crew with a copy of the completed film.
   Let them take pride in their contribution.

7. Never make your cast wait around on the set to shoot their scenes.
   Schedule each character's call time when you will be ready to use them; shoot their scenes and then allow them to go home.

8. Never allow negative people on your set.
   Negatively based people always bring the energy of everyone down.

9. Keep all aspects of your production simple.
   The more simple your production, the easier it will be to see it through to completion.

10. The basis for your film should be fun.
    Filmmaking is a creative process. All creative processes should be based in enjoyment. Don't let filmmaking become a job. Allow it to remain a free and happy pathway to the fulfillment of your creative dream.

FADE OUT.

THE ZEN

www.ingramcontent.com/pod-product-compliance
Lightning Source LLC
Chambersburg PA
CBHW070445090426
42735CB00012B/2467